MW01001707

New Hampshire
AND THE
Civil War

—— Voices from the Granite State ——

New Hampshire

AND THE

Civil War

—————— *Voices from the Granite State* ——————

BRUCE D. HEALD, PhD

FOREWORD BY WILLIAM HALLETT

Charleston   London

THE
History
PRESS

Published by The History Press
Charleston, SC 29403
www.historypress.net

Copyright © 2012 by Bruce D. Heald
All rights reserved

Cover photos courtesy of the New Hampshire Historical Society,
Concord, New Hampshire.

Unless otherwise noted, all images are from the author's collection.

First published 2012

Manufactured in the United States

ISBN 978.1.60949.628.9

Library of Congress CIP data applied for.

Notice: The information in this book is true and complete to the best of our knowledge. It is offered without guarantee on the part of the author or The History Press. The author and The History Press disclaim all liability in connection with the use of this book.

All rights reserved. No part of this book may be reproduced or transmitted in any form whatsoever without prior written permission from the publisher except in the case of brief quotations embodied in critical articles and reviews.

Contents

Foreword

U sually when someone is asked to write a foreword to a book, it is to critique the writing of the book, to compare the subject matter to other books that are perhaps already in the public and to see if there's an audience for the book.

I was asked by Dr. Heald to read over his new book and see what I thought. In recent years, other books on the Civil War and the Granite Staters who participated have come up. Would this book offer something new?

The Civil War is now 150 years away from our point of view. In that space of time, books on battles, armies, politicians, medicine, guns and machinery, generals, heroes, villains and more have covered the subject in so many ways that it's difficult to imagine any new perspective or new information coming to light that the public hasn't already learned or could learn in an existing book. Many so-called new books are just rehashed and retold versions of the stories already presented to us. A new cover, new photos and good marketing can find that old story back and sounding fresh. But to find something truly new and unique is what those of us who enjoy learning about the Civil War are constantly looking for.

This book takes on the story of the Civil War from a more personal level. Bruce Heald managed to gather the stories of many New Hampshire soldiers and sailors, using their own words from letters and diary entries. Heald strings their stories together to tell the accounts of the war itself.

How can I critique Dr. Heald's writing when his writing is sparse? What compels us to read this book are the experiences the men from New

Hampshire wrote about. Subjects like camp life and the adjustment to an army routine, battles with peril inches away, life in hospitals or in prison camps afterward that present their own risks—these stories are what we enjoy. Hidden for decades, many of these stories would still not be known if not for Bruce Heald's work in letting the soldiers and sailors tell them in their own style and in their own words.

Most of the stories are, with few exceptions, from men from New Hampshire. For many years, it appeared that study on the Civil War focused on states like New York, Pennsylvania or Virginia. However, in recent years, the role of New Hampshire has not only surfaced but has also shown that the state is able to hold its head up high, proud of what its sons did in fighting for the Union.

The book we have before us brings us a personal connection with New Hampshire during the Civil War as we listen to the voices.

William "Bill" Hallett
Author, *Newburyport and the Civil War*

Acknowledgements

I would like to thank the following individuals, companies and historical societies that have made their history and material available: the Cook Memorial Library, the Conway Library, Robert Cottrell, the Meredith Historical Society, William Hallett, the New Hampshire Historical Society, Douglas P. Knight, the Lewis Historical Society (1927 collection), New Hampshire Veterans Association, Richard D. Schubart, the Sanbornton Historical Society and the T. Faith Tobin private collection.

Introduction

The Northern Cause

Fierce rhetoric abounded between the states as to whether new territories entering the United States would be free or slave states. Debate surrounding the economic right or moral wrong of this issue, as well as states' rights to secede, raised a great deal of animosity between the Northern and Southern states to such a pitch that in April 1861, the Confederates States of America made a move to fire upon Fort Sumter, South Carolina. On Sunday, April 13, 1861, Civil War was declared.

President Lincoln framed the Civil War as a noble crusade in order to save democracy and determine its future throughout the world. His noble concept of the war did much to mobilize the Northern states, and New Hampshire joined that crusade. Little did anyone know what the magnitude of the war would be and the tragic effect it would have on the citizens of America. Four long and bloody years were to follow those first shots on Fort Sumter.

"A house divided against itself cannot stand," Lincoln predicted; he knew a constitutional crisis would bring either the triumph or the demise of slavery. This was an issue well engraved in the people of the nation: "I believe this government cannot endure permanently half slave and half free. I do not expect the house to fall—but I do expect it will cease to be divided. It will become all one thing, or all the other."

When President Lincoln called for seventy-five thousand troops to defend the Union and suppress the Southern insurrection for three months in order to suppress the rebellion, New Hampshire responded with an alacrity unsurpassed by any other state. The state sent into service eighteen volunteer regiments of Infantry, three companies of riflemen who participated in the First and Second United States Sharpshooters, the First New Hampshire Volunteer Battery of Light Artillery, a battalion for the First New England Volunteer Cavalry, the First New Hampshire Volunteer Heavy Artillery and additional men who served in the navy and marine corps. The New Hampshire regiments, which enlisted for three years, were usually engaged in battle.

The New Hampshire soldiers who fought in the War of Rebellion made great distinction of service, which we hold with pride for their participation to preserve the Union. New Hampshire furnished a total of 10,657 recruits for the infantry, cavalry and field artillery organization originally provided by the state in 1861. The majority of these first recruits were forwarded to the thirteen infantry regiments, which enlisted for three years of service.

In 1862, Colonel Edward E. Cross of the Fifth New Hampshire Volunteer Regiment proudly announced at Antietam: "The enemy is in front and the Potomac River is in the rear. We must conquer this day, or we are disgraced and ruined. I expect each one will do his duty like a soldier and a brave man. Let no man leave the ranks on any pretence. If I fall leave me until the battle is won. Stand firm and fire low. Shoulder arms! Forward march!" Colonel Cross was killed at the Battle of Gettysburg in 1863.

New Hampshire has every reason to be proud of its participation in the Civil War and its men who served. This book has assembled and preserved many rare historic letters, pictures and memories of the many soldiers of the regiments from New Hampshire. Let us cherish the special moments and the events that celebrate the valor and pride of the New Hampshire soldiers during the Civil War.

During this time of turmoil before the Civil War began, Abraham Lincoln sought the Republican presidential nomination in 1860. Lincoln had a personal interest in visiting New Hampshire, for his boys were attending the Philips Exeter Academy in Exeter, New Hampshire. While he was campaigning throughout New England giving speeches, many people, particularly Southerners, did not believe when he promised, not "directly or indirectly, to interfere with the institution of slavery in the States where it exists." It was Lincoln and Northern leaders who believed that, like living in a world still ruled by kings and princes, the collapse of the American Union might destroy for all time the possibility of a democratic republican government. "We can not escape history," Lincoln eloquently declared. "We shall nobly save, or meanly lose, the last best hope of earth." Lincoln made it clear that secession was unconstitutional but that the North would not invade the South. A young Union recruit put the issue simply: "If our institutions prove a failure…of what value will be house, family or friends?"

It was during the month of March 1860, while campaigning for the presidency, that Abraham Lincoln took some time to visit with his sons and write this rare letter to his wife during these troubled times:

Exeter, N.H. March 4, 1860
Dear Wife:

When I wrote you before I was just starting on a little speech-making tour, taking the boys with me. On Thursday they went with me to Concord, where I spoke in day-light, and back to Manchester where I spoke at night. Friday we came down to Lawrence—the place of the Pemberton Mill tragedy—where we remained four hours awaiting the train back to Exeter. When it came, we went upon it to Exeter where the boys got off, and I went on to Dover and spoke there Friday evening. Saturday I came back to Exeter, reaching here about noon, and finding the boys all right, having caught up with their lessons. Bob had a letter from you saying Willie and Taddy were very sick the Saturday night after I left. Having no dispatch from you, and having one from Springfield, of Wednesday, from Mr. Fitzhugh, saying nothing about our family, I trust the dear little fellows are well again.

This is Sunday morning; and according to Bob's orders, I am to go to church once to-day. Tomorrow I bed farewell to the boys, go to Hartford, Conn. and speak there in the evening; Tuesday at Meriden, Wednesday at New Haven—and Thursday at Woonsocket R.I. Then I start home, and think I will not stop. I may be delayed in New York City an hour or two. I have been unable to escape this toil. If I had foreseen it I think I would not have come east at all. The speech at New York, being within my calculation before I started, went off passably well, and gave me no trouble whatever.

The difficulty was to make nine others, before reading audiences, who have already seen all my ideas in print.

If the trains do not lie over Sunday, of which I do not know, I hope to be home to-morrow week. Once started I shall come as quick as possible.

Kiss the dear boys for Father.
Affectionately,
Lincoln

Chapter 1

Regimental Call to Arms

No state was more ably represented in Washington, D.C., when Lincoln went there to take the reins of government than New Hampshire. According to the state records, New Hampshire sent 31,650 enlisted men and 836 officers to battle in the Civil War. Of these troops, 1,803 enlisted men and 131 officers were killed or wounded.

The first men who went to enlist usually entered the service as members of militia companies. These organizations were for the most part military only in name, with their peacetime activities rarely going beyond holiday parades and ceremonial functions. Of later recruits, some entered into the regular army, while others went as substitutes. The majority of those who wore the blue entered the army as members of the volunteer regiments, which were formed under the auspices for each state and mustered into Federal service for periods ranging from three months to three years.

Mass meetings were the major feature of recruiting efforts. Those attempting to organize units would solicit recruits by personal appeal, broadside and advertisements in newspapers. Once a nucleus was signed up, the recruits were put to the task of bringing in other recruits.

Induction into Federal service, preceded in most cases by muster into state troops, was the first step of the recruits' early camp lives. After being formed by company, the men and officers were inspected individually, following which they were required to take the oath of allegiance as prescribed in the tenth article of war. Next came the reading of the article of war. Many times, reading the articles preceded the swearing in, as stated by a new recruit: "May 1861: The fact that nearly all violations…called for the death penalty or some other severe punishment so depressed a number of the boys that six of them hurriedly made their exit and were not thereafter heard of in connection with the company."

The parting words of many relatives to their soldier sons were, "Send me your picture."

The first complement to go from the state was the First Volunteer Regiment, which enlisted for three months in response to the proclamation issued on April 16, 1861, by President Lincoln. Major Sturtevant, the city marshal of Concord, put up a recruiting tent in back of the statehouse. More than two thousand men responded to the call. The first regiment was completed, and the rest went into the second regiment. These men were obtained in five days, and every thirty days thereafter, one thousand men were sent until sixteen regiments had been raised and sent south to Washington.

It is interesting to note that of the 12,713 original members of the thirteen New Hampshire regiments for the three-year term of service, 733 were Irish immigrants. Of the 9,986 recruits provided by the state, 1,858 were native Irish.

FIRST NEW HAMPSHIRE VOLUNTARY INFANTRY REGIMENT

The First Volunteer Regiment began to arrive at Concord on the fairgrounds of the Merrimack River, the camp being christened Camp Union. From May 1 to 7, the regiment was mustered into service for its country. On May 25, the regiment boarded the cars for Washington amidst the cheers of the local citizens. At Manchester and Nashua, the soldiers were greeted with similar demonstrations.

New Hampshire Fights the Civil War, by Mather Cleveland, MD, introduces us to Reverend Stephen G. Abbott, who wrote:

> *All the troops were anxious to engage the enemy as long as the army advanced, though the terms of enlistment of some of them would expire within a week. There was no sign of discontent until the retreat to Charlestown began. The truth seems to be that General patterson, who had distinguished himself in two war, wished to attack but that he was persuaded to retreat by too cautious military advisors, one of them Fitz John Porter. There was probably a want of confidence in the steadiness of the volunteers and militia among these regular army officers. They failed to take into account that there was no greater steadiness to be expected in the enemy's troops.*

The New Hampshire Volunteer Infantry Regiment answers the call, 1861.

Even if it had been undesirable to bring on a pitched battle there can be but little doubt that if Patterson's troops had been brought up in close contact with Johnston's, the latter would not have ventured to march away.

The First Volunteer Regiment did not engage in any fighting except the exchange of shots at intervals for two days across the river at Conrad's Ferry. The regiment did, however, do a large amount of guard duty; thus, the regiment faithfully did all that was required of it.

On August 2, 1861, the First Volunteer Regiment, with its ninety-day enlistment period having expired, was mustered out of Federal service at Sandy Hook, Maryland. The regiment returned to Concord, where it was paid and mustered out of state service on August 9, 1861.

It is interesting to note that after the First New Hampshire Volunteer Regiment was disbanded, about 60 percent of its members reenlisted in other New Hampshire regiments. The ninety-day period of service of this regiment was considered a period of basic training for these men who went on to become soldiers for the state of New Hampshire.

SECOND NEW HAMPSHIRE VOLUNTEER INFANTRY REGIMENT

Most of the original members of the Second Volunteer Regiment were enlisted for three months' service under President Lincoln's first call to arms; many of them were among the earliest recruits in April 1861. The surplus of men at Camp Union was sent to Camp Constitution, in Portsmouth, for the purpose of forming the Second Volunteer Regiment. But early in May, while the regiment was still in camp at Portsmouth, orders were received from the War Department to send no more three-month troops. Most of the men thereupon enlisted for three years, this second muster by companies dating from June 1 to 8. The regiment left Portsmouth on June 20, arrived at Boston on the same day and arrived at New York on June 21.

The regiment opened the fight at the first Battle of Bull Run on July 21. Being the first in the field of battle, the regiment saw more service than any other. The regiment spent nearly all its time in Virginia, where more blood was spilled than in any other state in the Union. The Second Regiment marched over six thousand miles and participated in nearly thirty battles. The regiment's loss was reported as seven killed, fifty-six wounded and forty-six missing.

The roll of the Second Volunteer Regiment originally contained more than three thousand troops. Every regiment but two from the state was supplied with officers from its ranks, and more than thirty regiments in the field had on their rosters names of men who were once identified with it.

The Second Regiment was involved in twenty-two engagements. The highest casualties came at the Battle of Gettysburg, 47; Second Bull Run, 36; and Williamsburg, 21 men. The totals for the Second Regiment were 2,555 served and 350 lost in service. The regiment was mustered out on December 19, 1865.

THIRD NEW HAMPSHIRE VOLUNTEER INFANTRY REGIMENT

The Third Volunteer Regiment was the second to be raised in the state for a three-year term of duty. On July 31, 1861, an order was issued by the governor offering a bounty of ten dollars to be paid to each man who had enlisted or might enlist and be mustered into the Third Regiment. The same order was carried into effect in recruiting for other regiments to be enlisted.

VOLUNTEERS WANTED!

In pursuance of a Proclamation by the President of the U. States, and by order of the Gov. of N. H. the

Third Regiment of Volunteers

within the State of New-Hampshire, will be enlisted for three years, unless sooner discharged by proper authority, to be held in readiness for service whenever called for.

In accordance with the above, and acting under the orders of the Governor of this State, I have opened a

RECRUITING OFFICE

AT

UNION-HALL BUILDING, COR. MARKET & HANOVER STS.

PORTSMOUTH,

for the enlistment for three years, of able-bodied men. None will be received who are under the age of eighteen, or over the age of forty-five. All under 21 will be required to bring a written consent from their Parents or Guardians.

Volunteers who shall be accepted will be uniformed, armed and equipped, when mustered into the service, at the expense of the State, and their pay will be the same as that of the corresponding rank in the Army of the United States, to commence at the date of enlistment.

GEORGE W. TOWLE, Recruiting Officer.

PORTSMOUTH, N. H. July 22, 1861.

Left: VOLUNTEERS WANTED. Join the Third Regiment of Volunteers. July 22, 1861, Portsmouth, New Hampshire. *Courtesy of the New Hampshire Historical Society, Concord, New Hampshire.*

Below: A group of men of Company H, Third New Hampshire Volunteer Infantry Regiment, Hilton Head, South Carolina, March to April 1862. *Courtesy of the New Hampshire Historical Society, Concord, New Hampshire.*

The Third Volunteer Regiment was organized and mustered in on August 23, 1861, at Concord for a three-year commission. The regiment was organized at Camp Berry on the intervale nearly opposite the southerly part of Concord and on the easterly side of the Merrimack River. Enoch Q. Fellows, of Center Sandwich, was selected to be its colonel. He was a West Point graduate who had been with the First New Hampshire, and he possessed excellent military skills.

On September 14, 1861, the regiment was ordered to Washington, where it arrived on the sixteenth. The men set up camp east of the Capitol.

During the four years' service on the east coast of South Carolina, Georgia, Florida, Virginia and North Carolina, the Third Regiment was engaged in sieges, battles, reconnaissance and skirmishes. During its term of service, the regiment had on its rolls 1,717 enlisted men, including 44 noncommissioned officers and band members and 101 officers. Of these, 190 were killed in battle or died of wounds, 137 died of disease, 196 deserted and 740 were discharged, 300 by expiration of term and 440 by disability. In January and February 1864, 270 of the regiment reenlisted. The regiment was discharged from service on July 25, 1865.

FOURTH NEW HAMPSHIRE VOLUNTEER INFANTRY REGIMENT

About two hundred men were left over in organizing the Third Volunteer Regiment, and they were ordered from Concord to Manchester to form the nucleus of the Fourth Regiment. The regiment was mustered into service at Manchester on September 18, 1861, just two weeks after the Third Regiment had left the state. Company A was enlisted at Dover, Company B at Nashua, Company D at Laconia, Company F at Great Falls, Company H at Salem and Companies C, E, G, I and K at Manchester. The regiment left Manchester for Washington on September 27, 1861.

The regiment was in two expeditions against Fort Fisher, the first under General Butler and the second under General A.H. Terry.

In April 1863, the men of the Fourth moved on siege operations against Morris Island and Forts Wagner and Gregg in South Carolina. Later, on September 7, 1863, they were involved in the capture of both Forts Wagner and Gregg. During the remainder of the year, the Fourth Volunteer Regiment was stationed at Hilton Head, South Carolina, for amphibious operations with the Third and Seventh Volunteer Regiments

Morning detail. The Fourth New Hampshire Volunteer Infantry Regiment going to its work at Hilton Head, South Carolina.

against Charleston. When the Fourth Volunteer Regiment returned to Manchester, it was given a magnificent reception by Governor Frederick Smyth and the citizens of Manchester. At that time, 140 troops returned in the regiment, and 50 were mustered out in hospitals. This unit lost 234 men killed in action or died of disease, and 57 died in Southern prisons. The regiment was discharged from service on August 23, 1865.

Fifth New Hampshire Volunteer Infantry Regiment

The Fifth Volunteer Regiment was organized at Concord, and the men enlisted for three years. Colonel Edward E. Cross of Lancaster was appointed colonel on August 27, 1861. It is written that the regiment camped east of the Merrimack River, near the lower bridge, and the camp was named Camp Jackson. The troops were mustered into service on October 26, 1861, and reported ready for active duty. The whole regiment numbered 1,010, including a fine band and a corps of buglers attached to each company, and left the state for the war effort on October 29, 1861.

Colonel Edward E. Cross, Fifth
New Hampshire Volunteer
Regiment.

According to Hobart Pillsbury's *New Hampshire in the Civil War*:

> *The one regiment in all the Union armies, which sustained the greatest
> loss in battle during the American Civil War, was the Fifth New
> Hampshire Infantry…It served in the first Division, Second Corps. This
> division was commanded successively by Generals Israel Richardson,
> Winfield Scott Hancock, Barlow, and Miles; and any regiment that
> followed the fortunes of these men were sure to find plenty of bloody work
> cut out for it. The losses of the 5th New Hampshire occurred entirely
> in aggressive, hard, stand-up fighting; none of it happened in routs or
> through blunders. Its loss included 18 officers killed, a number far in
> excess of the usual proportion, and indicates that the men were bravely
> led. Its percentage of killed is also very large, especially as based on the
> original enrollment. The exact percentage of the total enrollment cannot
> be definitely ascertained, as the rolls were loaded down in 1864, with the
> names of a large number of conscripts and bounty men who never joined
> the regiment…Known to the corps and division commanders as a reliable
> regiment, it was the more often called upon to face the enemy's fire, or
> assigned to the post of danger.*

During the three years and nine months that this regiment was in service,
it bore upon its rolls the names of about 2,600 men. It lost from casualties

Recruiting poster for the Fifth Regiment of New Hampshire Volunteers, Portsmouth, New Hampshire, July 22, 1861.

about 1,500, about 1,300 of whom were during actions. In addition, 16 of its officers were killed or mortally wounded in battle.

Instances of individual gallantry on the part of the officers and men in the Fifth Regiment are so numerous that a list of them would be too great for present listing, and a roll of its killed in battle would appear almost incredible.

The Fifth Volunteer Regiment was actively engaged in numerous major battles, including Antietam, Fredericksburg and Gettysburg, to name a few. A total of 1,051 men were lost during service. The regiment was discharged on July 28, 1865.

SIXTH NEW HAMPSHIRE VOLUNTEER INFANTRY REGIMENT

The Sixth Volunteer Regiment was recruited mainly in the western part of the state, under the same call with the same bounty as was paid to the three preceding regiments. The regiment organized at Keene and camped on the Cheshire Fairgrounds, about a mile and a half out from the city, at a camp

Arrival and departure of Federal soldiers. "The Front," 1861–62.

named Camp Brooks. At the camp, the regiment was mustered into service on November 27, 28 and 30, 1861, and left the state for active service on December 25 with 1,024 officers and enlisted men. Soon after the arrival of the Sixth Regiment in Washington, D.C., the troops were assigned to General Ambrose Burnside's division and were sent to Hatteras Inlet, North Carolina. The regiment was actively engaged in many battles and a number of reconnaissance and skirmishes. For many days during the campaign in the Wilderness, and for several weeks before Petersburg, the regiment was constantly under fire and lost a great number of troops.

While the regiment was at Roanoke and Hatteras Islands, the men were drilled and practiced as sharpshooters, and they were considered the best shots in the Ninth Army Corps. At Bull Run, the regiment recorded losses of 210 out of 450 men.

The Sixth Volunteer Regiment was discharged on July 17, 1865. It retired its service on July 22, 1865, and arrived at Concord, where it was given a formal reception by the state and its citizens. The men were immediately paid for their service and discharged. The regiment lost a total of 418 men during service.

SEVENTH NEW HAMPSHIRE VOLUNTEER INFANTRY REGIMENT

Colonel H.S. Putnam, Seventh New Hampshire Volunteer Regiment.

The rendezvous of the Seventh Volunteer Regiment recruits was established at Manchester on September 2, 1861. It was the understanding from the very beginning that the governor and council would commission such officers as were designated by General Joseph C. Abbott. General Abbott was commissioned as lieutenant colonel. Daniel Smith of Dover was major, and Andrew H. Young of Dover was among others selected for the regiment. The organization was fairly well completed, and the officers and men all mustered into service on December 14, 1861. By January 14, 1862, the regiment had left New Hampshire under orders to proceed to New York City. While in service, they were comparatively inactive, relieved only by an occasional dress parade or drill in one of the city squares.

The raising of the Seventh was regarded somewhat in the light of an individual enterprise and was therefore surrounded by many difficulties, but its success was thought by some to be quite doubtful.

Colonel Abbott was in command until the summer of 1864, when he was promoted to brigadier general. After the war, he moved to North Carolina and became a United States senator in 1871.

From the regiment, 320 men and 22 officers returned. Of these, fewer than 100 were among those who had left the state with the regiment in January 1862. Of the original field and staff, only 1 remained. The regiment lost a total of 426 men during service and was discharged on July 17, 1865.

EIGHTH NEW HAMPSHIRE VOLUNTEER INFANTRY REGIMENT

The Eighth Regiment was organized at Manchester and was mustered in on December 23, 1861. The Eighth Regiment was raised at the same time as the Sixth and Seventh, and the men who enlisted to make up its quota were paid the same bounty, ten dollars, by the state as those in the five preceding regiments.

This infantry was better known as the First New Hampshire Cavalry from December 16, 1863, to February 29, 1864, and as the Second New Hampshire Cavalry from March 1 to July 25, 1864

The Eighth Volunteer Regiment began early in the month of September 1861. The first company went into Camp Currier at Manchester on October 12, and on December 9, the regiment was full. This camp was named after Moody Currier, a member of the Governor's Council who later became governor of New Hampshire. On January 25, 1862, the regiment was transferred to Fort Independence in Boston Harbor.

Hobart Pillsbury records the following:

> *On February 16, six companies under the command of Colonel Hawkes Fearing, embarked on the ship E.* Wilder Farley, *destined on the Butler Expedition to reach Ship Island in the Mississippi Sound. On the 18th day of February the four remaining companies, Lieutenant-Colonel O.W. Lull commanding, left for the same destination on the ship* Eliza and Ella. *On March 18, 1862, the first named arrived at Ship Island; and on March 29, the* Eliza and Ella *anchored at the rendezvous, and the regiment pitched it camp two miles from the landing.*

The Eighth Volunteer Regiment was actively engaged in seven major battles. In addition to these, the regiment was engaged in fifty-three skirmishes.

On January 1, 1865, the troops and recruits of the Eighth remaining in service were organized under the direction of Brigadier General Brayman into three companies and designated as the Veteran Battalion, Eighth New Hampshire Volunteer, with Captain Landers as commander. The regiment lost a total of 360 men during service and was later transferred to the Second Light New Hampshire Cavalry on December 1863.

Ninth New Hampshire Volunteer Infantry Regiment

The Ninth Volunteer Regiment began recruiting in May 1862, and by July 31, most of the recruits had been mustered in at Camp Colby in Concord. The regiment was completed by August 23. After the Eighth Regiment had

A view of the Union Volunteer Refreshment Saloon, Philadelphia.

been sent to the field, recruiting in the state ceased, and by order of the War Department, all recruiting officers for volunteers were closed. In May 1862, an order was received from the War Department requesting New Hampshire to furnish an additional regiment of infantry. A bounty of twenty dollars was offered, which was subsequently increased by the state to fifty dollars for each person who might enlist in any new regiment and sixty dollars to those who would enlist in either of the regiments then in service. On September 14, 1862, three weeks after leaving New Hampshire, the regiment was engaged in the Battle of South Mountain.

According to historian Hobart Pillsbury:

> The record of the 9th New Hampshire is one of arduous campaigns, followed by comparative rest.
>
> It suffered in battle at Antietam and Fredericksburg, and in the mud at Falmouth; was cheered by the comforts of Newport News, and feasted in Kentucky; had its ranks depleted by disease in Mississippi, and returning to the Blue Grass region, recuperated for the hazardous march, over the mountains of East Tennessee. At Annapolis it welcomed recruits and convalescents, in preparation for the bloody ordeals of Spottsylvania, the "Mine," and Popular Spring Church, and the wearisome waiting before Petersburg.

Colonel Enoch Q. Fellows, a native of Sandwich, resigned as colonel of the Third Regiment in order to accept this command. Later, he was succeeded by Colonel Herbert B. Titus of Chesterfield. The regiment lost a total of 409 men during service and was discharged on June 10, 1865.

TENTH NEW HAMPSHIRE VOLUNTEER INFANTRY REGIMENT

The Tenth Volunteer Regiment was organized on July 1, 1862. One company was recruited at Nashua, one at Portsmouth, one at Andover and Wilmot, one at Farmington and Dover and the largest in Manchester. Captain Michael T. Donohoe, of the Third Regiment, was appointed colonel, and Honorable John Coughlin resigned his seat in the New Hampshire legislature to accept the appointment as lieutenant colonel of the regiment. The state bounty of fifty dollars was continued to all new recruits in order to avoid the impending draft.

Manchester was selected as the rendezvous at Camp Pillsbury. The named companies began to arrive on August 20, and on September 5, 1862, the regiment was mustered into service.

On September 22, the regiment left Manchester via rail and arrived at Washington on September 25. On the evening of the twenty-sixth, the regiment crossed the Potomac River to set up its base at Camp Chase, in Arlington Heights. It became assigned temporarily to Casey's Division, Defenses of Washington, D.C.

Both the Tenth and Thirteenth Volunteer Regiments served at Fredericksburg, Falmouth and Portsmouth, the Army of the James, Drewry's Bluff, Cold Harbor, the Battle of Fort Harrison, Fair Oaks and countless others. The regiment lost a total of 195 men during service and was discharged on June 21, 1865.

ELEVENTH NEW HAMPSHIRE VOLUNTEER INFANTRY REGIMENT

The Eleventh Volunteer Regiment was recruited in August 1862. The companies of the regiment, under the command of Colonel Walter Harriman of Warner, were mustered into service in Concord from August 28 to September 3, 1862. The regiment consisted of 1,006 officers and enlisted men.

Regimental Call to Arms

The Eleventh Volunteer Regiment was engaged in the following battles: Fredericksburg, Vicksburg, Jackson, East Tennessee, the Wilderness, Spotsylvania, North Anna, Cold Harbor, Weldon Railroad, Poplar Grove Church, Hatcher's Run and Petersburg. The regiment lost a total of 297 men during service.

The regiment was mustered of service on June 4, 1865, and arrived at Concord on June 7, 1865.

Twelfth New Hampshire Volunteer Infantry Regiment

The Twelfth Volunteer Regiment was mustered into service at Camp Belknap on the Concord Plains on September 10, 1862, and left directly for Washington. The regiment was known as the "sons of the soil," for they represented the brawn, if not the brain, of the state's mountains and hills. They soon received the title the New Hampshire Mountaineers.

The regiment was active at Fredericksburg, Chancellorsville and Gettysburg. The regiment served in the Armies of the Potomac and the

Field and line officers of the Twelfth New Hampshire Volunteer Regiment. *Courtesy of the New Hampshire Historical Society, Concord, New Hampshire.*

James, where, by a loss of more than one-third of its members, it made for itself a distinguished record of valor and sacrifice unsurpassed by any other regiment of infantry in the Union army. In the final chapter of this book, a detailed diary is given of Freedom Sanborn, a Twelfth Regiment soldier.

The regiment lost a total of 320 men during service and was discharged on June 21, 1865.

THIRTEENTH NEW HAMPSHIRE VOLUNTEER INFANTRY REGIMENT

The Thirteenth Volunteer Regiment answered the president's call of July 1, 1862, for an additional 300,000 troops. The Thirteenth Regiment was commanded by Colonel Aaron F. Stevens of Derry. Two companies were formed in Rockingham, Hillsborough and Strafford Counties and one each in Grafton, Merrimack, Carroll and Coos. All enlisted came to Camp Colby, near Concord, between September 11 and 15, 1862. Enlistment was completed on September 23, 1862.

The regiment at first consisted almost entirely of Native Americans and New Hampshire's representative young men, many of them descendants of the Patriots of 1776 who fought in the Revolution.

Much of their service was with the Tenth Regiment, as listed earlier. The regiment lost a total of 181 men during service and was discharged on June 22, 1865.

FOURTEENTH NEW HAMPSHIRE VOLUNTEER INFANTRY REGIMENT

The Fourteenth Volunteer Regiment was the last long-term regiment to be furnished by New Hampshire. It was filled mostly with residents of the four western counties. The regiment was organized at Concord and was mustered into service on September 24, 1862.

The regiment, with 968 officers and enlisted under Colonel Robert Wilson, left the state on October 18, reached Washington on the twentieth and camped in shelter tents on East Capitol Hill. An immediate assignment to Grover's Independent Brigade sent the regiment into active service defending the Potomac, above Washington, against guerrilla attacks. The regiment made four sea voyages of fifteen thousand miles and served in seven Confederate states.

The colors of the Fourteenth were waved over Fort Sumter when Robert Anderson again raised the flag he had hauled down four years before.

The regiment lost a total of 232 men during service and was discharged on July 8, 1865.

FIFTEENTH NEW HAMPSHIRE VOLUNTEER INFANTRY REGIMENT

The Fifteenth Volunteer Regiment was mustered into service in the statehouse yard at Concord on November 12, 1862. On the morning of November 13, the regiment proceeded, by way of Worcester and Norwich and the Norwich line of steamers, to New York. The regiment marched from the boat to Long Island. Here, the regiment joined the forces of the secret expedition of N.P. Banks, which was destined for New Orleans and operations on the Mississippi.

A view of Company G of the Fifteenth New Hampshire Volunteer Infantry in Concord, New Hampshire.

During their time of enlistment, the members of the Fifteenth Regiment were under orders to Port Hudson in the early summer of 1863 and remained there through two major assaults. The regiment suffered a great deal from sickness. From July to August 13, 16 men died, leaving only 480 men fit for duty.

After leaving Port Hudson for New Hampshire, 50 men were left on the account of sickness, many of whom died. The regiment lost a total of 161 men during service and was discharged on August 13, 1863.

Sixteenth New Hampshire Volunteer Infantry Regiment

The Sixteenth Volunteer Regiment was mustered into service on November 1, 1862. The regiment was under the command of Colonel James Pike, who had been a member of Congress and a Methodist minister.

The regiment posted itself around Port Hudson and then sailed down to New Orleans. It held the city of Brashear and later a fort in the defense of New Orleans. In six weeks at the fort, the regiment was reduced from 600 guns to 216.

The regiment lost a total of 221 men during service and was discharged on August 20, 1863.

Seventeenth New Hampshire Volunteer Infantry Regiment

On August 4, 1862, the State of New Hampshire was required to organize three regiments, one in each of the congressional districts of the state, with the understanding that the officers and recruits enlisted in the three districts were to belong to the Fifteenth, Sixteenth and Seventeenth Regiments of New Hampshire, respectively. On October 23, 1862, Colonel Henry O. Kent, of Lancaster, was appointed commander of the Seventeenth Regiment. According to historian Hobart Pillsbury:

> The 15th and 16th left the State in the month of November 1862. Colonel Kent's regimental organization occupied the camp vacated by the 15th, and continued there under his command from the 19th day of November, 1862, until the 16th day of April, 1863, excepting while a portion of the men were furloughed to save expenses. Great exertions were made to fill the regiment by

State of New-Hampshire.

Adjutant General's Office,

Concord, Nov. 6, 1863.

To the Selectmen of *Meredith*

    In apportioning the number of volunteers required from this State, under the late call of the President for "300,000 volunteers," your quota, calculated on the enrollment of the first class, made by the several Provost Marshals of this State, is 26.

    The call of the President is made, regardless of the deficiences of States or districts, upon former calls and apportionments. No computations can be entered into with the respective cities or towns for any alleged deficiency or surplus of volunteers furnished prior to the date when the Government draft commenced in this State. To avoid a second draft these troops must be raised and mustered into the United States service on or before the 4th day of January next.

    It is earnestly hoped that the quota of New-Hampshire may be furnished, by volunteering, in season to supersede the necessity of another draft. To accomplish this requires the united efforts and co-operation of every true and loyal citizen of the State. Shall the men be furnished? Let every possible effort be made, and the work will be done.

                          Daniel E. Colby,
                                   Adjutant General.

A letter from the selectmen of Meredith, New Hampshire, from the state of New Hampshire requesting volunteers for active service for the war effort, November 6, 1863. *Courtesy of the Meredith Historical Society, Meredith, New Hampshire.*

Colonel Kent, who was an able, accomplished, and popular officer; but owing to the extreme depletion of the arms-bearing population of the State and the necessity of filing the ranks of the older regiments, which was continually being done, it was found to be impossible to thus complete his regiment.

Subsequent to the organization of the 15th and 16th regiments, one full company and part of another, in all about 125 men, were added to the 17th Regiment from the other Congressional districts, who with the 791 men belonging to Colonel Kent's regiment, as enlisted from the Third District, would have made the total number under his command 916 men— considerably more than the number entitling him to muster into the service of the United States as colonel of the regiment.

The regimental organization was well disciplined, drilled and instructed of the command commenced and adhered to. In December, it was decided to postpone the state draft, and orders were issued to reject all substitutes applying for enlistment on the unfilled quotas. On February 9, 1863, officers and men of the Seventeenth Regiment were furloughed until April 1, at which time the command again reported in camp, cheered by the official assurance that the regiment would be at once filled, in order to participate in the spring and summer campaign of 1863.

About this time, orders were received by Governor Berry from the secretary of war to consolidate the Seventeenth and Second Regiments, under such regulations as he might prescribe. On April 16, 1863, this order was carried into effect. The officers and the noncommissioned officers of the regiment were mustered out, and the enlisted men transferred. The failure to fill and forward the Seventeenth Regiment was in no way attributed to its officers and men. The men proved to be excellent soldiers and behaved so well at Gettysburg as to elicit a special order of commendation from the colonel of the regiment at the expiration of their term of service.

Eighteenth New Hampshire Volunteer Infantry Regiment

Six companies of the Eighteenth Volunteer Regiment were raised under the call of the president on July 19, 1864. On October 4, 1864, they joined the Engineer Brigade commanded by General Benham at City Point, Virginia, and Colonel Charles H. Bell of Exeter was commissioned commander of the regiment.

According to Major Otis F.R. Waite:

> *The quota of the State having been filled at the organization of the six companies, no further companies were raised until the next call for troops. Which was made on December 21, 1864. The remaining companies were now commenced, and on the 17th of January 1865, Major Thomas L. Livermore of the Fifth, who was at the time serving on the staff of Major General Humphries, was commissioned Colonel.*
>
> *During the months of February, March and April, three of the new companies joined the regiment. As soon as the tenth company had been*

The State of New Hampshire.

A PROCLAMATION.

BY HIS EXCELLENCY JOSEPH A. GILMORE,
GOVERNOR OF THE STATE OF NEW HAMPSHIRE.

THE General Government has determined to put down the Rebellion by the Fourth day of July next. By a Proclamation of the President of the United States it is—

"ORDERED, That a draft of 500,000 men to serve for three years, or during the war, be made on the 10th day of March next for the military service of the United States, crediting and deducting therefrom so many as may have been enlisted or drafted into the service prior to the first day of March and not heretofore credited."

New Hampshire, having filled her quota under the call for 300,000 volunteers, will need to raise only her proportion of 200,000 men, in order to meet all demands upon her before the tenth of March. By telegram from the War Department I am informed that this call "is equivalent to a call for 200,000 men in addition to the 300,000 called for, October 17th, 1863." The quota of New Hampshire under this last call has not been officially announced, but will be, in round numbers, an advance of 67 per cent. on the quotas of each town as assigned under the call of October 17th, by circular from the Adjutant General's Office, bearing date November 9th. The whole number of men required of our State to meet the present call will not be far from 2000. A detailed statement of the additional men required from each town will be issued from the Adjutant General's Office as soon as possible.

Meanwhile I would urge upon the people of New Hampshire the importance of taking prompt and decisive measures to meet this new demand upon them. The Government bounties will not be paid after the first of March next; but till that time each fresh recruit will receive from the General Government $300.00; each man who has seen nine months service, $400.00. By the advice and with the consent of the Executive Council, I do hereby declare that the State bounty of $100.00 to soldiers enlisting in New Hampshire Regiments will continue to be paid up to March 10th, 1864.

In order to meet this new requisition I am authorized by the War Department to recruit the four companies of New Hampshire Cavalry which have recently been attached to the First R. I. Cavalry to a full Regiment which shall be known hereafter as the FIRST NEW HAMPSHIRE CAVALRY. This affords the sons of New Hampshire an opportunity to enrol their names in a regiment which is to be made up of picked men and will doubtless be assigned to special service. An accomplished officer of the regular army has already been detailed by the War Department to assist in the organization of this Regiment.

Re-enlistments under the recent call from members of New Hampshire Regiments which have seen two years service will be credited to the quota of their respective towns, or any other town which they may prefer within the limits of the same Congressional District. Each man re-enlisting from these old Regiments will receive $400.00 Government bounty and $100.00 State bounty, and have the privilege of spending 30 days with his family. Many members of the 2d, 4th, 5th and 6th regiments of infantry, the Sharp-shooters and the N. H. Battery have already re-enlisted, and will be credited under their new call, as our quota of 3768 men under the call of Oct. 17th, 1863, was filled at home, without counting these re-enlistments.

The men from New Hampshire can be raised by volunteering, and I am determined they shall be. By filling up the New Hampshire Cavalry to its maximum and encouraging the hearty disposition of our glorious veterans to re-enlist we shall meet all requisitions upon us by the 1st of March. I am confident that we shall do this. There will never be another draft in the old Granite State. Her sons will rise in their might and like an avalanche from their icy hills sweep the last traces of armed treason into the Gulf of Mexico before another return of our great national anniversary. Only one more effort and the thing is done.

Given at the Council Chamber in Concord, this first day of February, in the year of our Lord one thousand eight hundred and sixty-four and of the Independence of the United States the eighty-eighth.

JOSEPH A. GILMORE.

By His Excellency the Governor,
ALLEN TENNY, *Secretary of State.*

A proclamation by His Excellency Joseph A. Gilmore, governor of New Hampshire—a call for 300,000 volunteers. *Courtesy of the Meredith Historical Society, Meredith, New Hampshire.*

BY HIS EXCELLENCY JOSEPH A. GILMORE,

GOVERNOR OF THE STATE OF NEW-HAMPSHIRE.

A PROCLAMATION.

TO THE PEOPLE OF NEW-HAMPSHIRE.

I am informed by telegraph from Washington, on the authority both of the Secretary of War and the Provost Marshal General, that our State will be accredited with all men furnished under the draft of July 3, 1863, while no account will be made of men called for under that draft. As a consequence of this decision, I am happy to say that New-Hampshire is in excess of all demands upon her at the present time.

Our deficiency at the beginning of the present official year, was	388
Quota called for October 17, 1863,	3,768
Quota as estimated under call of February 1, 1864,	2,512
Total,	6,668
Men furnished under the draft,	3,012
Men furnished under call of Oct. 17th,	3,768
Re-enlistments from old regiments not reckoned as a part of our quota under the call of Oct. 17th,	387
Total,	7,167

In addition to the re-enlistments already reported at the Adjutant General's office a number of men have been mustered as veterans from the Third, Seventh and Eighth Infantry and the N. H. Cavalry, and these are yet to be credited to the State. It is not too much to hope that New Hampshire is at the present time at least 600 men in excess of all demands upon her. It is certain that her quota under every call is full.

While this cheering news relieves us from the necessity of any especial exertion to avoid a draft in the Old Granite State, let me appeal to her patriotic citizens to keep the balance on the right side. Other calls may be made upon us, and in meeting them New Hampshire must still head the column. Let us send into the field in the Spring a full Regiment of Cavalry, composed exclusively of the sturdy yeomanry of our own State. As an incentive to continued effort in this direction, I do hereby announce that the State Bounty of $100.00 will continue to be paid, till further notice, to citizens of New Hampshire, who enlist either as fresh recruits or veteran volunteers to the credit of towns in which they have residence. The bounties offered by the General Government of $300.00 for fresh recruits, and $400.00 for veterans will be paid up to March, 1, 1864.

Given at the Council Chamber, in Concord, this ninth day of February, in the year of our Lord one thousand eight hundred and sixty-four, and of the Independence of the United States the eighty-eighth.

JOSEPH A. GILMORE.

BY HIS EXCELLENCY THE GOVERNOR WITH THE
ADVICE AND CONSENT OF THE EXECUTIVE
COUNCIL.

ALLEN TENNY, Secretary of State.

A proclamation to the people of New Hampshire by His Excellency Joseph A. Gilmore, governor of the state of New Hampshire. *Courtesy of the Meredith Historical Society, Meredith, New Hampshire.*

mustered into service, Colonel Livermore was mustered, and joined his regiment on the 8th of April.

The engagements of service was at Port Hudson and Baton Rouge, Fort Steadman, Petersburg and the capture of Petersburg.

The regiment lost a total of forty-one men during service and was discharged on July 29, 1865.

FIRST NEW HAMPSHIRE VOLUNTEER HEAVY ARTILLERY REGIMENT

On July 22, 1863, the First Regiment Volunteer Heavy Artillery raised a full regiment of twelve companies and was mustered into the companies stationed at Fort Constitution and later ordered to Washington and assigned to duty under Major General Auger. During the winter of 1864–65 and until the muster out of the regiment, it garrisoned a line of earthworks ten miles long in the defense of Washington. The duty of the regiment was important to the safety of the Capitol.

FIRST NEW HAMPSHIRE VOLUNTEER LIGHT BATTERY

The state of New Hampshire furnished only one light battery, which was recruited entirely in Manchester in 1861. It was mustered into service on September 26, 1861. The company consisted of a six-gun battery of rifled brass pieces, with 155 men and 115 horses.

In June 1863, the battery moved as part of General Joseph Hooker's army against General Lee, making one march of thirty-two miles in twelve hours. On June 29, 1863, the battery saw action at Gettysburg located on the Cemetery Hill. It lost four men, three horses and one gun. When General Lee retreated back to Virginia, the battery moved with the rest of the army across the Potomac River.

On May 6, 1864, the battery took part in the Battle of the Wilderness and at Po River, Spotsylvania and North Anna River. On June 3, it also fought at Cold Harbor and proceeded to the siege of Petersburg. On September 25, 1864, fifty men and four officers of the regiment were mustered out. Forty-two reenlisted.

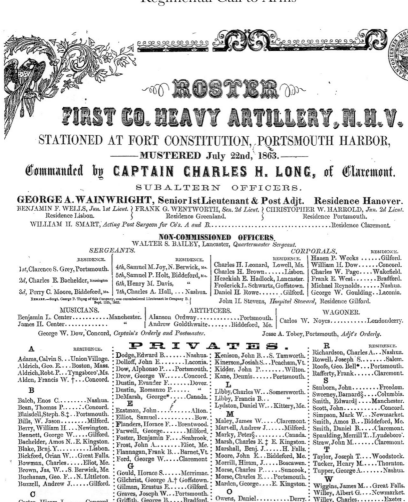
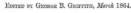

Roster of the First Company of Heavy Artillery, New Hampshire Volunteers, July 22, 1863. *Courtesy of the New Hampshire Historical Society, Concord, New Hampshire.*

FIRST NEW HAMPSHIRE VOLUNTEER CAVALRY REGIMENT

The First New England Cavalry was the first full regiment of the service to be raised in the spring of 1864 in New England. The regiment was composed of three battalions; the first and third were enlisted in Rhode Island and the Second in New Hampshire.

The regiment was organized and mustered into service in the fall and winter of 1861 at the fairgrounds near Concord, where it remained until December 22. The New Hampshire battalion joined the two Rhode Island battalions at Pawtucket, Rhode Island, on January 22, 1862, when the regimental organization was completed. All the companies in the organization were ordered to Washington. They reached there on April 25, 1864, and established themselves at Camp Stoneman, at Giesborough Point.

A major battle for this regiment was located at Cedar Creek, Virginia, on August 12, 1864. The battle represented here was considered a skirmish with the retreating Confederates. The regiment lost a total of 147 men during service and was discharged on November 9, 1865.

FIRST NEW HAMPSHIRE VOLUNTEER SHARPSHOOTERS REGIMENT

New Hampshire furnished three companies of sharpshooters for the Union army service: E, F and G. On June 15, 1861, a regiment was raised for a ninety-day term of service.

Recruiting offices were opened throughout the state, and on September 9, 1861, the first company was mustered into service in Concord, with Amos B. Jones as captain. Two days later, the unit was ordered to Weehawken, New Jersey; on September 15, 1861, it was ordered to Washington with the companies that had arrived there and joined the First Berdan's United States Sharpshooters. General Hiram Berdan's U.S. Volunteer Sharpshooters were involved in thirty-six engagements, including Gettysburg, Cold Harbor and the Wilderness.

New Hampshire and the United States Navy

The U.S. Navy was little prepared for the advent of the Civil War. Many of its commissioned ships were obsolete. In the States, only four warships were available for duty, and most of the trained seamen came from New England. According to the naval records, the United States owned ninety ships that carried 2,415 guns at the beginning of the war; the forty-two commissioned vessels in the fleet carried only 555 guns.

Above: Captain John A. Winslow and the officers on the deck of the man-of-war USS *Kearsarge*, 1861. *Courtesy of the New Hampshire Historical Society, Concord, New Hampshire.*

Opposite: Sharpshooting, a trial of skill of Berdan's Riflemen before General McClellan and staff at Washington.

The Third New Hampshire Band, Hilton Head, South Carolina, February 1863. *Courtesy of Mather Cleveland, MD,* New Hampshire Fights the Civil War.

The Regimental Band, Hilton Head, South Carolina, February 10, 1863. *Courtesy of Mather Cleveland MD,* New Hampshire Fights the Civil War.

By the end of the war, the United States Navy was considered the strongest naval power in the world. The war revolutionized the science of naval warfare through its new technology, thus making other navies throughout the world obsolete.

In 1861, when the declaration of war was issued, the Union navy made ready to authorize the construction of sixteen large sloops of war, including the USS *Kearsarge*, which was named for one of New Hampshire's mountains. In January 1863, the 1,031-ton *Kearsarge* was commissioned. The ship was supplied with eight guns, including two eleven-inch Dahlgren pivot guns mounted amidship, which allowed it to take large areas with 135-pound shots.

The Third New Hampshire Band was organized in Concord and was mustered into service on February 10, 1863, under the direction of Gustavua W. Ingells of Concord. The band was stationed at Hilton Head, South Carolina, and was held in high esteem by the commanding officers.

"I can assume that you and every member of your band, stands in the highest estimation of every one in this department from Major General Gilmore down. We never expect to see such another as Ingell's Post Band here again. Signed: W.T.M. Burger, Assistant Adjutant General, Hilton Head, South Carolina."

The band was mustered out on July 4, 1865.

Chapter 2

Soldiers' Encampment

I started in this thing a boy; I am now a man.

The recruit soon became proficient in firing and maintaining his weapon, taking care of his equipment and living outdoors. He learned to kindle fires, cook rations and boil coffee. If the recruit survived the many camp diseases that devastated Civil War armies, he soon became accustomed to the discipline and regimen of camp life. Daily duties were issued to him and regulated him in his training. Drill was the main occupation of the soldier, for only by becoming proficient in parade ground maneuvers could he manage the necessary movements on the battlefield.

A large number of New Hampshire soldiers who served with the Union in the state of Louisiana died of typhoid fever and dysentery, and some were incapacitated by malaria. It may be worthwhile reading some of the remarks of the soldiers on matters of flies, mosquitoes and drinking water. Claude Goings wrote from Ship Island on April 30, 1862: "The flies are too damned thick for anything. We always manage to keep a few cartridges with which we blow them up. There is a hole in the top of our tent, which we keep nearly all the time here. We put 4 or 5 charges of powder on a plate set it down on the ground and touch it off and the way the flys go up through the hole is fun for white folks."

Warren Knowlton, Third New Hampshire Volunteer Regiment, Company D, wrote to his brother on September 5, 1861, from Camp Sherman, Mineola Long Island, New York:

Brother James,

I suppose you would like to hear from me. We left Concord Tuesday morning, arrived here Wednesday night had rather a hard time as it was rainey and cold all night. We are all well with 2 or 1 exceptions. There was a report that three men were lost over board but can not find out for sertanty that it was he.

There is to be a Division as Brigade formed here under the command of Sherman. We are the first Regiment on the ground. It is a pleasant location here. Tel the folks that U am well and in good spirits. I am lying flat on the ground writing.

I hear that olde Jeff is dead is that so?

Write and let me known how thinks prosper Direct.

Warren Knowlton
Camp Sherman
3rd NH Vol Co D
Mineola Long Island, NY
Yours VC

A later letter reads as follows:

Washington September 1861.
Friends at Home,
I think quite likely you know that the NH 3rd left Long Island before this. We left Saturday night about 9 PM arrived at Baltimore Sunday night about dark. Marched through the City without any trouble. By the way we had mints of a time when we was at Philadelphia, as that we should have a time going through Baltimore but instead of a row the people sound well disposed towards us. I have not heard the pleasure of seeing Ole Abe yet.

Don't feel much like writing now. I will let you know more about us by and by.

I am able and On good spirits with the exception of being tired and sleepy—Write direct to:
Warren Knowlton
NH 3rd Vol. Co. D
Washington DC

Three unknown officers from the Third New Hampshire Volunteer Regiment at Hilton Head, 1862. *Courtesy of the New Hampshire Historical Society, Concord, New Hampshire.*

Knowlton continues his correspondence home on October 17, 1861, with the following message:

Annapolis Wednesday Oct. 17
Friends and all other folks at home.
I now take this opportunity to let you know how the 3rd Regiment is going.
We left Washington soon after I wrote last. I received Jases letter the next day after arriving at Annapolis. Was happy to hear of course, received a letter from Thomas and one other about the same time. We have orders to sail this week or the first of next, where to we don't know, but down the coast towards Dixey I presume. There is 75,000 troops in the expedition bound down South to clear them out down there.
It seems that Gov Dix took a great fancy to our Reg't and Col. Fellows. I understand that the Gov and Col. tried to keep this Reg't here, but Maj. Gen. Sherman would not give us up.
We had a beautiful flag presented to us yesterday, which is the second that we have received since we left the Old Grand State.

I have not much time to write now. You must excuse me if I don't say much. We are all well with few exceptions.
Yours in haste—
Warren Knowlton
PS O received that paper. Was very glad to see a NH paper once more.

James Wiggin of Tamworth wrote this letter from Camp Lander on January 19, 1862:

Dear brother and sister, Willard and Sarah.
I received yours & Hannah & Henry's letter last Wednesday night with much pleasure. I was happy to hear from you all. I suppose you all are done looking for me home now. I have given up the idea all together, I never was so fat in my life I am nothing but a bloat. I weigh 160 lbs and am gaining every day. I have gut so I do my duty now with ease. I can't lift much on account of my rupture, but I can handle a lusket with any of them, unless I am sick again. I shant go home until the way is settled. I live out here first rate an well contented. Our company has moven down to the river. We had to build log huts to live in we are in the woods. I shall be a wild man by the time I get home. I should not know how to act in a house now.
Well a soldier's life is a gay one—Willard, we had some baked beans this morning—they went good only I wnted some brown bread to go with them.
Willard, I expect you will see a man from my company in your house next week if he goes. I shall send by him for some thing that I am suffering for. He is the man that I sleep with nights he and I has put a little hut together. It is McNeals, he is a good man I tell you. I will forward all the news when he goes if he does and I think he will. I must write a few lines to Henry, Hannah. I have no particular new to write so this will be for you to. I shall send for you to send me out something that will do wont if tell Foly will write to her soon.
I received 8 papers with the letter and I was glad to get something to read. Willard—I am greatly obliged to you for papers that you send me.
Good Bye,
James B. Wiggin.

On June 20, 1862, Claude Goings wrote from Fort Macomb:

Now I think the people of N.H. are quite intelligent but they don't know but a damned little about mosquitoes. We have bars here for the purpose of keeping them out of bunks but fasten it out as tight as we can, they are bound to come in and often times the whole Co. will be up all night. Some swearing some singing while others are dancing. In short impossible to keep them off.

According to historian Mather Cleveland in his *New Hampshire Fights the Civil War*:

The 8th New Hampshire Regiment remained at Ship Island through April until early in May 1862 when three companies of the Regiment under Lieut. Colonel Lull, were sent to Fort Macomb, about twenty-five miles from New Orleans, to guard the southern entrance to Lake Pontchartrain. The remaining companies of the 8th New Hampshire Regiment were transported to Camp Parapet near Carrollton, Louisiana, where the detachment from Fort Macomb joined them early in July 1862. The Regiment spent the summer with a heavy schedule of drill. Claude Goings wrote on July 22, 1862:

"The soldier might live through this season without much danger of Cholera or fever if they were taken care of but there is no mercy or reason about our Commanding officers and we are obliged to drill 5 hours per day which is more than we ever drilled at the North. The men care but very little whether they learn anything or not, all they care is to get to their quarters where they can rest."

James Wiggin of Tamworth wrote this letter from his encampment on August 24, 1863:

Dear Sister & Brother

I received your letter last night with the rings in don't you think that I gut it quick only 2 days and a half on the road those rings suits my fancy to a charms. I have them in but they like to tore my ears all to pieces and was so hard to bend but I have them in and they can never get out without help. I am very much obliged to you indeed for sending them. They are a very nice pair. I am sorry to hear that Kate Smith is married. I had my cap set on her, now there is no one else that I can think of except old Hannah Drew and I don't hardly fancy her. She is to old. I received a letter from mother last Saturday and I wrote to her yesterday they were all well. There is not much signs of a move for a present here we are filling up Our regiment with conscrips. I have no particular new to write. McNeal is well he is in the Brigade commissary department—he sends his love to all. Hannah owes me a letter you wrote for me to take things as easy as I could not break

Soldiers' Encampment

*myself down I bet so but I can't help but being brock down for I am now a
soldier on any consideration they can't help but giving me mine in one year
since just 2 years ago today as I as sworn in at Lynfield all I shall be afraid
of what I do get home that they will draft me again but I had rather loose a
leg or an arm than come out here gain after I have survived 3 years. well I
will close…give my love to little Foly, tell her I look at her picture every day
I would like to see Willards hand writing once more. Willard I would like
to talk dutch with you for 2½ hours—I think I could wax you.*
Well good bye,
From Jim.

An impressive number of regiments from the northern part of New
Hampshire found Southerners to be lazy and indolent. One soldier in the
Fifth Regiment wrote: "The men are very lazy, too lazy to work themselves
but willing to sit around the store-doors whittling, smoking, and drinking…
The money comes from the labor of women of all ages from fifteen to fifty
years and upwards, in the fields, hoeing, plowing, and planting."

On another occasion, a soldier from the Third Regiment wrote of having
seen some splendid houses but added:

*With all the elegance and appearance of wealth, there is an air of shiftlessness
around, hardly perceptible at first, but which never fails in forcing itself on
you after looking closely. There is a paling out here, a window-blind hanging
by one hinge there, a gate propped up with both hinges gone; and I have seen
in some of the finest dwellings a sunbonnet, or something else with ruffles on
it, stuck into the window where a pane of glass is broken.*

A New Hampshire soldier of the Nineteenth New Hampshire Volunteer
Regiment, from Massachusetts Company K, wrote the following letter to his
brother in Tamworth, New Hampshire, from Fortress Monroe, Harrison's
Landing, Virginia:

Brother Willard
*I rote to Hannah the other day and I rote I was not very well and I am still
on the failing ground. I am afraid I will be sick again and I want a box of
something that I can't get here. I would like some lemons and sugar to make
a drink—the water is poor here and I can't drink it without something in
to take away the taste and I would like some of Sarah's doughnuts and the
most I want is some cherry brandy on cherry, rum to curre the diarrhea I*

have it very bad and I can't do any duty. Willard, stuff is so high here that it costs me all I can earn to by stuff that I kneed. And Willard, I would like some of this cocoa that comes in papers to drink I can make it out here. I would like a towel, Will. If you will forward them I will reward you well if I ever get out of the army.

Willard, go down to the market and let jerry fix the box up for you he had rather do it than not and he can put in the lemons. Willard, I don't care how much they charge you send I would give $5.00 for a pint now.

Willard, pack it so no one can find it out for some of the boxes are broke open and theirs is taken out. Willard, I was happy to have a letter from you when McNeal came out. I will answer it soon you spoke about going up in old Tamworth. I wish I was there to go we would have a time and a half. Well, give my love to Sarah & Hannah & Foly and Johnny Kate & Mary and ms Davis Chapin howe & Jerry. Tell them I will answer their letter I received by McNeal. I was pleased to hear from them. Will direct the box to Harrison's Landing va via Fortress Monroe and please forward. Write me a letter when you send the box so I can look out for it.

James Boynton

A soldier from the Twelfth New Hampshire Volunteer Regiment relates the following to his sister on January 10, 1863, near Camp Falmouth:

Dear Sister
I will answer your letter now that I received 5 days ago. I shall have rote before but I have been down to Aquia Creek to work and just got back. I am well and hope you are the same. I got through the battle of Fredericksburg safe and sound and unhurt glory to got for that. I never was so sick of anything in my life as I am of the war. We are all played out intirely. But there will be a forward movement again soon.

This war never will be settled by fighting. Sarah, McNeal has just come back to the regiment he has been gone 6 months soon. Ted Willard I am a bold soldier boy. Sarah, have you got a case of instruments that I sent home by one of our boys. Sarah, I want you or Hannah to knit me a pair of gloves and send to me in a paper all the boys have them. All most freezes hold of the musket. I must close good By my love to all.
James
Cynthiana Key, Oct. 25th

Another soldier from the Fourth New Hampshire Volunteer Regiment relates the following to a family friend in Manchester:

Mr. Kingsbury
Dear Sir,
I received a merry welcome letter from you a short time since enquiring about
James. I should be glad if I could give you any information in regard to him
but I fear what little I know about him will give you little satisfaction. We
left Sniders Bluff August 8th and stayed at Helena the 12th it was nearly
dark when we stoped. (we stoped every night) the supply of coal being short
they took on a fresh supply which they had to carry right by where James
and myself were laying with the rest of our Co. the officers said some of
us would have to move when James said that he was not very well and he
would go and find him and other place
    To day he went off and I saw nothing more of him. The boat started
the next morning before light and when I awoke we were steaming up the
Miss. I expected James back there but as he did not come I began to look for
him in different parts of the boat and not finding him. I made enquiriery
about him but could learn nothing. The Helena is the place you spoke of
we stoped there a few minutes when we went down there was an ILL Regt
there when they probably had a hospital to their Regt, but I think there is
no general hospital there. I can not say as regards the size of the place as
I did no go up in to it at that time. All boats had stoped there and if any
soldiers was acsidently left they were obliged to take them up. I do not know
as James had any enimes at least none who would push him over board.
None of our officers have made any efforts to look him up. I think there is a
post office in Helena. I do not know the name of person there. There were
few of our men went ashore there as it was dark when we stoped there. I
think there was nothing to hinder any from going ashore. there was a plank
laid from the boat to the bank to go ashore on. My health is good we are in
good place here and I am in hopes that we should stay some time.
Yours with much respect.
Samuel

RATIONS

The camp rations were primarily hardtack, soup and coffee. An unknown
soldier wrote the following lines describing the food:

The Soldiers' fare is very rough
The bread is hard, the beef is tough;

If they can stand it, it will be,
Through love of God, a mystery.

Midway through the war, in April 1863, this verse was published in the *Nashville Daily Union*, and it appeared that the daily allowance of rations for our soldiers was

> *twelve ounces of port or bacon, or one pound and four ounces of salt or fresh beef; one pound and six ounces of soft bread or flour, or, one pound of hard bread, or, one pound and four ounces of corn meal; and to every hundred rations, fifteen pounds of beans, or peas, and ten pounds of rice or hominy; ten pounds of green coffee, or, eight pounds of roasted coffee, or, one pound and eight ounces of tea; fifteen pounds of sugar; four quarts of vinegar... three pounds and twelve ounces of salt; four ounces of pepper; thirty pounds of potatoes, when practicable, and one quart of molasses.*

The Union soldiers were not regularly issued fresh vegetables in the field; however, they did have the opportunity to acquire them by foraging.

The cook's galley for Company H, Third New Hampshire Volunteer Regiment, Hilton Head, South Carolina, April 1862. *Courtesy of Mather Cleveland, MD,* New Hampshire Fights the Civil War.

Soldiers' Encampment

Between the lines during a truce.

Sometimes they received what was referred to as "desicated compressed mixed vegetables."

The army bean was an important staple food in the Union camps. New Englanders particularly were fond of beans. A typical recipe would consist of the following:

> *Take as many beans as you want for a mess and par boil them then take a spade and dig a hole large enough for the pot you are going to cook the beans in and build a fire in it as warm as you can, then take the pot of beans, and put a piece of meat in the center of the pot then cover to pot over and put it in the hole covering the pot with the coals that are in the hole and shovel earth on top of them and in twenty four hours you have a soldiers dish of baked beans.*

The Southern climate inspired a considerable amount of growling. It is not at all surprising to find sarcastic allusions to the "Sunny South" in letters written by homesick soldiers from New Hampshire. The following is no exception, written by Tim to his brother in Meredith, New Hampshire, from near Sabrine Crossroads, Louisiana:

April 14, 1864

Dear brother—I hope this letter finds you—God only know if the army wont make a mess out of postal delivery also. Everything else is in a bad way. The Jonnies don't move worth a damn and we couldn't catch 'em anyhow not with our command. A schoolboy would know that you can't flank in a swamp, and we are in a swamp. This entire "state" is in a swamp. Cursed country. It isn't worth fightin' for I tell you wat. This campaign's a mess, and it has rained constantly. As if the swamp didn't wet nuff. When we fight 'em they jess disappear, maybe we should just go on home and give em this mess. Lots of the lads are getting sick, but I am doin well. I managed to forage a right proper amount of snake bite medicine to ward off the chill of these damp cursedly dark nights. It is just light enough at night to make toe darkness visible. The wagon trains are always getting stuck and rations are a sometimes thing. Always hungry. An my damn tobacco got wet. This is a bad place to be. And bugs—lots of damn bugs and snakes. Hell, we can't fight what with all the distractions.

Have you ever seen a wagon in mud up to its axels? From real close, like right behind it? It was our squad duty to help the other day. Lazy bastard teamsters will never miss that whiskey. Providence blessed us boys with good fortune that day, and a ham from a fat bastard artillery co.—it was good. Mostly we all miss home, normal times seem very far away. And this will never end. I stand a better chance of getting to Andersonville than home the way we are led. They sure didn't mention this at the town hall on the broadsheet. If I ever make it home I'll get me that education and come back here and be the boss-man. HA!

These people are different. We took some Texas boys prisoners and we couldn't understand nothing they mumbled. And dumb as a stump one was. But he had dry tobacco.

Hope New Hampshire is as pretty as I remember it. I cannot wait to get home or away from this place. I don't mind fightin' but this isn't It is beyond belief. We couldn't be any more post now that if we were deaf dumb and blind. But that is our command know that wet wood don't burn worth a damn? And the people! The women looks like they been ridden hard and put away wet.

Lincoln should relieve Banks, or send him (alone) further west. We are only making 3 miles a day. Great Pursuit. "With whiskey and snuff on the ration, we'll never see another cold beer; I wish that General Banks would get us the ---- outa here" I think Vicksburg was far enough. Some of the boys in another regiment may have deserted. They never came back from Pickett duty—Bless them. This place isn't like Virginia, no

Horseshoeing in the army.

place to go that ain't already as bad as where you at. The Rebs say they got general starvation leading them an I told them I'd trade him for our general incompetence. All we do all day is march and stop, fall in, count-off, right face, halt. And for $13.00 a month. 47 cent a day. Hell, I could steel that much. I can't wait to see the sun again. Everything is rotting. Soon enough I'll be barefoot. Did Jefferson ever see what he was buying. You could not make hell any more miserable than Louisiana. We get maybe 3 hours sleep a night before the bugs wake you. Or the rains.

We chew coffee beans during the marches to stay awake and if there is a major fight, we wont be any good. I could sleep under an active cannon. Cold and wet and hungry about sum up this campaign. But not without humor—I treated they boys to my 14 filthy stanzas of Rosin the Bow last night and got a cigar for my trouble. I'm glad I didn't have to listen to me sing. I've often found that whiskey, when taken in large amounts of moderations makes me a fine baritone. At that point—who cares if it was raining again, or stiff.

Don't write cause we don't know how far this little trip will take us. I'll let you know when we are back to solid ground with all the comforts that the army can supply us with. Until I see you agin, my friend, I hope you are well and in good health—I remain
Your obedient servant,
Tim

The soldiers' diet. This was a typical campsite, where New Hampshire soldiers would gather around the makeshift campfire and cook whatever was available from government issue, from peddlers or from the land itself.

There seems to be little comfort for the weary soldier, but letters from home were well received. Caleb had to complain to someone!

St. Augustine, Florida March 17th 1865
Dear Sister
I received your very kind letter by the last mail and was very glad to hear from you so soon. My health is pretty good now. It has not been very good for the last two or three weeks past. I have had some kind of sore in my bowels, it has got most well now, it has not been so bad any time but what I have done my duty all the time.
You want to know what the Regiment thinks of politicks. They are all most Democrats. We had our election the other day. my company voted thirty six Democrats and six Republicans. When we left Manchester it was the other way but the Negro question has changed them. The Regiment is six eleventh Democrats now, We lost five of our men the other day. the Rebels stoped our advance picket but they all got away. We went after them and

had Glen Cab Abbott to command us and he would not let us do the first thing. They got five of our men and we only got three if them in return. Oh, I wish you could be out here just one day and see what we have to suffer from fleas, sand flies and mosquetoes. You ought to of seen me this morning when I come off of guard. The fleas had bit me so that the blood ran down my legs, and the sand flies had bit my face so that I could not see out of one eye. it was sweld six so and the other eye and the other eye was not much better. The mosquetoes are as big as most darn-needled are at the north. We have mosquetoes nets to put over our heads but we continue to get bit.

Paul sends his best respects to you. The air smelled the sweets here that ever you smelt the orange trees are just in bloom now and they smell like orange flowers.

What do the folks think of the Dame right labor? Do you think they will resist. I suppose Dale Ames will be a leaving a gain for Canada. How do the girls get along up there, I cant think of anything more to write so I will stop giving love to all of the folks.
Your loving brother
Caleb Dodge
HN 7th Regiment
St. Augustine, Florida

A soldier of the Eleventh New Hampshire Volunteer Regiment stationed in City Point, Virginia, wrote his sister the following on April 22, 1865:

Dear Sister and family,
It is a long time since I have heard direct from you, or written to you, not since I was at home, have been waiting for you to write first but have got tired of that, so am going to break the ice myself. It will be of little use for me to undertake to tell you of what has been transpiring since I came back to my Reg't. Your have read all about it in the papers, Now Petersburg, Richmond & the Army of Northern Virginia has all but surrendered to our Federal forces, since which time it has been one continual stream of rejoicing until the ascination of Lincoln, which seemed to create a dead silence over every thing, and every body. How very sad that he should be stricken down just at this time, when the day was just beginning to dawn on our beloved country, for which so much blood and precious lives have been lost, sick and dead is worst than any savage nation would think of perpetrating on their most bitter enemies The south will make nothing out of it, if it turns out that the leaders of the Southern Confedracy had any thing to do with it. Many of the paroled

prisoners seem to feel very bad about it, they seem to think they will be worse off, under the rule of Johnson than of Lincoln, which I hope may prove to be the case. This part of the country has been filled with paroled Rebel prisoners they surrendered their army, but most of them are getting off now. They seem to feel pretty sore about their late defeat—say they are ready to cave in when Bobbie does. Our Reg't has been very luckey of late, we were not in the hottest of the engagement on Petersburg April 2nd (for a wonder) did not lose a man. Since then we have marched as far as Burkesville junction. Were not at the front at the surrender of their Army. One week ago yesterday our Reg't was detailed to come to City Point, to guard Commissary Stores, going to Burkesville on the cars, a distance of 63 miles, Sunday I with 18 men were detailed to guard two trains. We returned Tuesday night having been gone 3 days and two nights. Had the cars and engine off track eight times, while we were gone. The road is terrible bad. (all played out like the Southern Confedracy.) Wonder what Robert would say if he had to run over such poor roads. I have heard him scold about rough roads in Vt., which were like glass compared with these. Yesterday we were relieved from this duty by a Reg't of the 5th Corps. The 9th Corps has been ordered to Washington, part of which has all ready embarked at this place. We are to join the Corps as soon as our Brigade arrive here. No one pretends to know what is to be done with us upon our arrival at Washington. I have a bit of a relic picked up on the battle field at Petersburg, Va., April 2nd 1865, which I will send to Robert. It is a Rebel Va. Yankey bullet, which met and were seeled together in one solid Union, an emblem of what our country will be when this war is closed. I have put a block of wood between them to keep them apart, as when found and marked them Reb & Yank, so that you may know which is which. They were actually fired from two guns, and met between the two lines, where they were picked up by Horace Sawyer of Co. E, 11th N.H., Vols. I never have seen but one other of the kind before since being in the service and never heard of but two. I have not heard from home, but some time. Folks were all well the last that I heard.

Since I saw you I have received a commission and been mustered into Co. E as 1st Lieut. For three years more of the men are all enjoying good health. Wm. And myself are fat and ugly as ever.

I do not think of much more worth writing, I have concluded not to send those bullets this time it is so heavy I am afraid someone will take them out, will save them and bring them to you some time.

Love to all, Write soon,
Your every true brothers
Solomon

Soldiers' Encampment

C. Dodge Jr. of the Eleventh New Hampshire Volunteer wrote his sister the following near Alexandria, Virginia, on May 10, 1865:

Dear sister Eliza,

I will try and write a few lines to you this eve in answer to your good long letter received last week, Tuesday morning. Just as I was starting to go over to Washington on business, I did not read your letter through till I was on my way back if I had I should have tried to have found cousin Frances Dodge but do not know as I should have succeeded in doing so, as I do not know what street they live on. I will give you credit of answering one letter as soon as received, I wonder what is going to happen when the time has come for one of our family to answer a letter as soon as received, would be very much pleased, if our folks at home were half as prompt. Think I should hear from there much often than I now do, have not heard from them for two weeks. If they are all dead, I should think they would write and let us know. You wrote that the papers seemed to talk as though the 9th A.C. was destined to some distant part of the country, but I have very little fear of that at the present time, if one can judge any thing from what he sees and hears, we are stoping here for the rest of the army to arrive, after which we are to have one grand review of the whole army of the Potomac, at least, then when that is over we are to go to our several states to be mustered out of the service of the "United States of America." Then will there be whaling and smashing of teeth over the chicken & turkey bones through out the Northern states. Then shall the fatted calf be killed and we will pick his bones around the beautifully laden tables of "Old New England."

I should have liked very much to have been at Northfield at the time of the great glorification over the fall of Richmond & Petersburg, but more particularly at the time when the old steady men began to "treat."

I presume that some of our folks have written ere this to you in rigard to what an exchanged prisoner belonging to the 7th N.H. Regt from Hillsboro, by the name of Carr, has told in request to cousin Caleb, and a cousin of his, who was there at the time of Caleb's death by the name of Dodge. The discription of who answers at very well to that of Juliam. Father has been to Hillboro to see Mr. Carr, and took Julian's photograph which he thinks is the one who used to visit Caleb in his last days. Oh! I am so much afraid that it may have been Julian that I hardly know what to say. Much rather would be known that he died on the battle field, than to know that he has been suffering in those hellish prisons all the time since he was missing, but still how gladly would I feel to know that he was safe once more in our lines, once more to return to his friends and home.

There is but little news of any important worth us, I have a Washington Chronicle, which I will send along with this, there is a very sensible letter in it from a "Soldier."

Have had some excitement in our quiet 11th Regt for the past few days before yesterday. Three Frenchmen stole $259.00 from another Frenchman all recruits. They were mistrusted to have done it, and were tied up by the thumbs to make them own up, which they did after hanging some hour and a half. They were told that they should hang until they were dead, unless they would confess and I guess they that so, but they stood the torture like heroes for a long time. Only 50 dollars of the money was recovered which was hid under a stump. 35 dollars was eaten by one of them after he was arrested before being searched. Charges have been preferred against them, and they have been sent to Division HdQ to await Court Martial. Yesterday three other men (recruits) were Court Marshaled for "absence without leave," the sentence is not yet been made known. This evening two other recruits got drunk and got to be fighting, one of them stabed the other with a knife a little fun once in a while just to pass away the time.

Wm. is with the wagon train, which is expected here soon, by the overland rout from City Point, he was well the last that I heard from him. My health is very good, am now in Com'd of Co. G, which I did not like to take very much and have the responsibility of all the property belonging to it I assure you.

I won't write much more. Give my love to Robert and the children, and a large lot to yourself, excuse my poor scratching and spelling.

Write soon. Good by, your every loving & true brother,
C. Dodge Jr.

Chapter 3

Regimental Battles

This was the ultimate test of soldiering. Nothing was more important to the closing of opposing forces in the rebellion. In this war, however, fighting was an intimate element for survival. The enemy could be seen with the naked eye, and contests usually culminated in head-on clashes of yelling, shooting, striking masses. Closing with the enemy was more than a figure of speech.

Upon the attack with the enemy, occasional references in official reports indicate "furious yells" and "wild cheers," suggesting that now and then the cry of the Union bore some resemblance to that of the Rebels. It is certain that the hurrahs that distinguished the Yankee cry were something shouted with savage abandon. Since the principal function of the battle cry was to relieve tension, it was usually spontaneous. But sometimes commanders specifically ordered their men to shout with the view of fighting the enemy. At Antietam, Colonel Cross of the Fifth New Hampshire added another detail:

> *"As the fight grew furious," according to one of his men, "the colonel cried out. Put on the war paint…Taking the cue…we rubbed the torn end of the cartridges over our faces, streaking them with powder like a pack of Indians, and the colonel to complete the similarity, cried our Give 'em the war whoop! and all of us joined him in the Indian war whoop."*

In the ensuing fracas, the whoopers were successful, and the man who told the story was inclined to give some credit to the savage makeup and shouting.

The Fourteenth New Hampshire Volunteer Infantry seen marching into battle.

Union troops attack Port Hudson. "Port Hudson will be ours today," announced General Nathaniel P. Banks on the morning of May 27, 1863.

Before the battle was decided, the regiment may have repeated the assault several times, as at Fredericksburg. Or they might have had the defensive role, as at Gettysburg, or else the contest might have taken the form of attack by one side and then the other, as at Shiloh.

Regimental Battles

Second New Hampshire Volunteer Regiment

Private Martin A. Haynes, Company I, Second New Hampshire Regiment, recalled the first major battle between the Union and Confederates at First Bull Run on July 21, 1861. The following letter was written from Washington on July 24, 1861:

The battle was the hardest fought so far, and the losses on both sides were heavy. At the roll call this morning, 175 were missing from the Second Regiment, but this number will doubtless be cut down as stragglers come in. Of my eight tent-mates, six went. Two [Harvey Holt and Henry Morse] *were killed outright and one* [George F. Lawrence] *was severely wounded in the head. I got a little upset at the very tail end of the fight. The regiment had crossed over to the opposite hill, and about a hundred of us had taken cover in a cut in the road. We had a house on our front, some secessionist cannon up near it, and enough of the enemy to give us a real lively time. There was a rail fence along the edge of the cut, and I rested my musket on one of the rails, and carefully sighted on a fellow who seemed to be showing off. Then something happened. A cannon ball struck the rail, one of the fragments hit me in the head and neck, and I rolled down the bank. I heard one of the boys cry out "Mark is killed!" and for about half a minute I didn't know but what I was. But when we had to break for the rear, a few minutes later, I had no trouble in keeping up with the procession.*

In all my life I never suffered from thirst as I did that day. On the advance, our regiment was right at the ford of Bull Run creek when the head of the column sighted the enemy. A staff officers rode back with the announcement and called to the men to fill their canteens. I waded up a few feet and filled my canteen with good clear river water. A little while after, I took a drink, spat out the tepid mouthful in disgust, and emptied the canteen. I learned my lesson and will never do that again. Before that day was over, I would have given dollars for one square drink of that same water. On the retreat I one time scooped up a few sips from a mud puddle which men and horses and wheels were ploughing their way. Before reaching Centerville I filled up clear to the ears from a little trickling rivulet, and filled my canteen as well. Laid down in the old bivouac and went to sleep. After two or three hours was waked up and told to keep agoing. The old thirst was on me, but when I lifted my canteen it was empty—drained to the last drop. If I could have got hold of that sneak thief the casualty list would have been one bigger, I think.

Private George H. Sargent, Company C, Second New Hampshire Regiment, wrote his letter from Washington on July 28, 1861, which described to his brother his Bull Run experience:

We were the first to go onto the field and the last to leave it. We had to fight hard. We were drawn up in a line of Battle, when a masked Battery began to play on us with great loss of our side. In a short time Riflemen opened on us, then our cannon began and we had it tough and tight, but after 4 or 5 hours we gained advantage and we kept it. We drove them from one of their Batteries at the point of the Bayonet. When they were reinforced by about 30 thousand fresh men and we had to retrete in hast. Out orderly of our Company and five others with about 30 of other Regts, went through or part way through some woods, we went through when we were on the way to Battle. We had got part through on our way back when we were surrounded by 200 Rebels when we broke away and ran for life. I got home the first one of our camp and call that a good days work, don't you? I guess that you would have given out if you had been me. Some of the men were taken prisoners. Rhurl Emerson is one, so I guess he will not write you very soon.

According to Mather Cleveland's account of the Second New Hampshire Volunteer Regiment at the Second Battle of Manassas (Bull Run): "After General Stonewall destroyed the supply depot at Manassas Junction on August 27, General Hooker's Division marched back to Centerville and on the 29th of August crossed Bull Run creek by the old Stone Bridge. The Second New Hampshire Regiment was back on the field where they first fought in July 1861."

Private Martin Haynes wrote from Alexandria, Virginia, on September 6, 1862, describing the assault of the regiment on the Confederate troops at Groveton:

We were ordered to advance through the woods, without any supports, and attack the rebels behind the railroad grade five or six feet high. We went in. They gave us a volley and we charged them, the Second going over the work with a yell and giving those fellows the surprise of their life. It was savage for a short time, but we were determined to drive them and we did. Then we went for the second line a few rods further on and set them agoing. And pretty soon it became apparent that what there was left of us were being surrounded. Then we got out. We had to be or be taken prisoners. We lost 147 men out of a little over 300 that went in and most of these within a very few minutes. General Grover said it was the greatest bayonet charge in the War. I got my first man as I went over the bank. A rebel threw his gun up aiming at somebody at my right. He never fired for I gave it to him from the hip and doubtless saved the life of so Second Regiment man. Just as I was starting on my return trip something tickled up upper lip and the roots of my nose and for a while I was doing the ensanguined act of the smallest capital of any man in the regiment. It was a pretty close shave all the same. One inch further in the wrong direction would have spoiled my beauty and three inches would have spoiled me. I do not know how soon we may be on the move but hope not for some time, for really the regiment is in pretty bad shape.

BATTLE OF ANTIETAM

Soldier accounts of combat were as varied as the personalities and experiences of the men who wrote them. A typical description of a battle was by one of our boys from the Fifth Volunteer Regiment, who wrote the following report of the Battle of Antietam to his father:

September 16–17, 1862
…The next morning we had our second battle—it was rather strange music to hear the balls scream within an inch of my head. I had a bullet strike me on the top of the head just as I was going to fire and a piece of shell struck my foot—a ball hit my finger and another hit my thumb. I concluded they meant me. The rebels played the mischief with us by raising a U.S. flag. We were ordered not to fire and as soon as we went forward they opened an awful fire from their batteries on us, we were ordered to fall back about a half-a-mile. I staid behind when our regiment retreated and a line of skirmishers came up—I joined them and had a chance of firing about 10 times more…Our Generals say they (the rebels) had as strong a position as could possibly be and we had to pick into them through an old chopping all grown up with bushes so thick that we couldn't hardly get through—but we were so excited that the "old scratch" himself—all loaded & firing as fast as he could see a rebel shoot at—at last the rebels began to get over the wall to the rear and run for the woods. The firing increased tenfold then it sounded like to the rolls of thunder—and all the time every man shouted as loud as he could—I got rather more excited then I wish again. I didn't

63

think of getting hit but it was almost a miracle that I wasn't the rebels that we took prisoners said that they never before encountered a regiment that fought so like "Devils" (so they termed it) as we did—every one praised our regiment—one man in our company was shot through the head no more than four feet from me, he was killed instantly. After the Sunday battle I took a carte of the wounded until 11 pm. I saw some horidest sights I ever saw—one man had both eyes shot out—and they were wounded in all the different ways you could think of—the most I could do was to give them water—they were all very thirsty. Our colonel was formerly a captain and he is just as cool as can be, he walked around among us at the battle to bullets flying all around us—he kept shouting to us to fire low and give it to them.

Your loving son

According to General Sturgis's report of the Fifth New Hampshire Volunteer Regiment, which served at Antietam: "The Regiment rushed at a double-quick over the slope to the bridge, and over the bridge itself, with an impetuosity which the enemy could not resist, and the Stars and Stripes were planted on the opposite bank amid the most enthusiastic cheering from every part of the field."

Fourth New Hampshire Volunteer Regiment

During the spring of 1863, the Third, Fourth and Seventh New Hampshire Regiments performed amphibious operations against Charleston, South Carolina. On April 13, 1863, Captain J.M. Clough, Fourth New Hampshire Volunteer Regiment, Company H, wrote the following from Hilton Head:

The expedition has turned out a perfect fizzle. We maid one of thos splendid retreats so often spoken of. We hear all kinds of rumors. One is hunter and Commodore Dupont could not agree. The Navy wanted to do all and get all the glory so there could be no cooperation. We could not land except under the guns of the Navy. Dupont would not help and if it was so I don't blame Hunter for withdrawing his troops for it would of bin a perfect Slaughter for us to of landed without their help. I for one don't think Hunter is the man for this department. He is not popular among the troops nor never has bin.

Regimental Battles

Also from Hilton Head on April 14, 1863, Corporal Charles H. Fullerton, Fourth New Hampshire Volunteer Regiment, Company E, wrote:

We have been on an expidishion to Charleston...we went to Stonno inlet arrived there Sunday [April 6] about ten o'clock. On Monday at three oclock the iron clad gunboats went into Charleston harber and commenced an atact on fort Sumpter. They faire about two hours and then holed off with the intencion of renewining the action the next morning but thare was orders arrived ffrom Washington not to fire agan in this department what it means we cannot tell. We lay at ancor all the time about nine miles from Charleston then we were ordered this plase and are now in camp. I hope this war will soon close so that we can com home to our folks but I should rather stay hear for ten years than to have the name of deserting. A man that will enlist and get a big bounty and then desert is just no man at all and he aut to be despised by every boddy.

On May 12, 1863, when the Fourth New Hampshire Volunteer Regiment had been moved to Folly Island, another soldier of the Fourth Regiment by the name of Private Ransom R. Wheeler of Company I wrote: "We get some news by way of the rebs we crossed the crick—thay say thay have no tea or coffee and we put it on a board and send it a cross to them the women comes down to the shore and begs for tea coffee shugar candles &c. they say they are very poor and are starving condition."

On July 18, 1863, Captain Clough of the Fourth New Hampshire Volunteer Regiment, Company H, wrote from Folly Island, South Carolina:

It was thought to take the Fort by storm so the brigade under General Strong made a most terrifick charge. Mounted the parapets of the fort and for a time held it but the fire was so terricick from Sumpter and the Infantry inside that our troops had to fall back with great loss. The 7th N.H. went in with 18 officers and came out with only four. Most of them supposed killed. Col. Putnam was shot through the head while leading the charge and died instantly. Gen. Strong reported mortally wounded. Gen. Sewmour was wounded finely.

During July and August 1863, the men of the Fourth New Hampshire Volunteer Regiment served as sappers under engineer officers digging advancing trenches toward Battery Wagner. Most of this work was done at night. Captain Clough, Company H, Fourth New Hampshire, wrote of this from Morris Island, South Carolina, in August 1863:

I am at the front nights to work. Tuesday night we had an awful night. At about one o'clock I had advanced 150 yards from our outer works towards Fort Wagner with rifle pits and at the extension erected works to put in four pieces of light battery to support infantry. After completing it we advanced a short distance and put in stockade to prevent the progress from an attack. The enemy saw us and amediately opened on us with grape and canister from Wagner. We fell into our trenches just completed an mediately came up to the 3rd N.H. to repel an attack. For three hours the firing was terefic. Our batteries amediately opened. Fort Sumpter went at it. The Monitors run up and pitched in but at daylight all became quiet. I had 150 men and we lay close in the trenches. Some times we thought we was in the middle of Versuveus. One case of grape from Wagner burst in our midst and wounded five of the 3rd N.H. that lay near me at the time—very near but still unhurt. The works that we still hold with Captain Brooks of the Engineers are nearer [Wagner?] *than any as yet.*

FIFTH NEW HAMPSHIRE VOLUNTEER REGIMENT

After the Fifth New Hampshire Volunteer Regiment returned to Falmouth on May 12, 1863, from the Battle of Chancellorsville, Lieutenant Hurd wrote:

I wish I were able to give you a description of our May party and excursion. Poor Frye and Folsom, I am afraid they will never again join our boys. The former we know nothing about but suppose him wounded and a prisoner. Folsom we know lost a foot and could not leave the field. We all came as near being taken prisoners that there was not much fun in it…Lt. Col. Hapgood does very well.

Private George E. Frye, Company E, Fifth New Hampshire Volunteer Regiment, was killed on May 3, 1863. Private Thomas T. Folsom, Company E, Fifth New Hampshire Volunteer Regiment, died of wounds on May 26, 1863, in the hospital near Aquia Creek.

Lieutenant Hurd, Company E, Fifth New Hampshire Volunteer Regiment, wrote of the dreary winter after Fredericksburg and the mud march on

The mud march. "The auspicious moment seems to have arrived to strike a great and mortal blow to the rebellion and to gain that decisive victory whish is due to the country." So announced General Ambrose Burnside to his Yankee soldiers on the morning of January 20, 1863.

January 27, 1863, from Falmouth: "The regiment remains about the same; a few die every week or two. I have only one man in the hospital here, Wm. Weston, and he is fit for duty all but his disposition. Private William Weston was wounded at Fair Oaks, Fredericksburg and Chancellorsville, but survived to be mustered out with the Regiment."

Seventh New Hampshire Volunteer Regiment

On March 13, 1863, Lieutenant Colonel Joseph C. Abbott of the Seventh New Hampshire Volunteer Regiment wrote from St. Augustine to Ira Mc L. Barton of Newport, New Hampshire, former captain of Company E, Fifth New Hampshire Regiment:

My dear Capt:
Major Henderson and myself in accordance with your request to the Colonel have embodied some of the circumstances and events connected with out Reg. From its formation up to the first of Jan. 1863. Owing to the fact that we have been in no action of importance we make but a small show, yet let me assure you the New Hamp. Has no Reg. In service

more thoroughly instructed, under better discipline, or which has more faithfully performed whatever duties have been laid in its way. Hoping that we may yet blazon something on our banners and with hopes for your speedy return to health.

I am yours very truly,
Joseph C. Abbott

EIGHTH NEW HAMPSHIRE VOLUNTEER REGIMENT

The first engagement of the Eighth New Hampshire Infantry was reported to be at Labalieville or Georgia Landing on October 27, 1862. In this engagement, the Eighth, with little over 400 fit for duty, had 12 killed and 32 wounded and took 170 prisoners.

Early in 1863, General Banks began to collect his forces at Baton Rouge for an advance on Port Hudson. On January 20, 1863, Claude Goings wrote from Baton Rouge:

My health is much better than when I wrote you last. I joined the Regt. At Camp Steavens Thibodeaux, about the 15th of December. Our Regt. was ordered to leave Camp Steavens December 30th and arrived here Jan 2nd. Our Army will soon be ready to move up the river to take Port Hudson, which is about 16 miles from here. The Rebels hava had two or three months to fortify the place and as usual will give us a warm reception and will doubtless welcome many of us to what they call Hospitable Graves.

On March 25, 1863, Goings wrote a letter describing the advance of the Eighth New Hampshire Volunteer Regiment on March 15 to the vicinity of Port Hudson and its return to Baton Rouge:

Then we came back about Sun Set, but only to get an order to pack up in 10. minutes. This was impossible but we got ready as soon as we could and started. We marched on 5. miles that Night but it was 11. ocl. When we halted. We started again at 4 in the morn. And During the Day we marched about 10. m. farther. And to within about 5. m. of Port Hudson. Here we were told by the Gen. would be the battle ground of the morrow. The thought of this would not have kept us awake much so tired and Hungry *had we got and forbid building any fired so we could not get any coffee. At 10. ocl. Nearly all had lain Down on the cold ground and were fast asleep. When the fleet opened fire on Port Hudson and so loud was the noise that Nearly all sprang to their feet. together we remained in readiness for action all Night but No enemy came out to give us Battle at about 11. ocl. The next morning we were ordered to fall in and Gen. Paine read an order from Gen. Banks. That During the Bombardment of last Night the Gunboats Hartford & Albatross had ran past the Batteryes of Port Hudson, and that the object of the expedition was aclomplished and we were ordered to retreat back again. We arrived Near the Spot where we halted the Night before and as it looked like rain we buisied our Selves fixing up a rude Shelter with our blankets. We had not been at work 10. minutes before it began to rain and with it came a regular tornado of wind blowing Down everything that we had contrived to keep the rain off. Darkness came on we were obliged to make the best of it. The rain continued all Night and not much Sleep we got I can tell you. We were in the edge of a swamp where on looking around in the morning we found ourselves unable to move without getting into the water. We remained in this miserable Swamp until Friday the 20th when we marched back Here to Baton Rouge.*

In December 1863, the Eighth New Hampshire Volunteer Regiment was converted to mounted infantry to serve in the projected Red River Campaign. Unofficially, the regiment was designated the Second New Hampshire Cavalry, but it remained the Eighth New Hampshire Infantry. The purpose of the Red River Campaign was to capture Shreveport, Louisiana, and open the way to Texas.

Sergeant Claude Goings, writing from Granico Landing, Louisiana, on April 18 and 19, 1864, described the action in the engagements:

I have just received your kind letter of March 21. I was very happy to hear you were all well. It is so seldom that you write that I had almost given up the thoughts of getting another letter from you. My Health is as good as usual. I suppose you will hear of our movements in this army ere you get this letter. However I will try and tell you something about it. We started from New Orleans the 2nd Day of March and have been on the tramp ever since until we came Here a few days ago. We came up with the enemys rear near Franklin and kept up a continuel chase of their army until the 7th of April when they having received reinforcements gave us battle. And a tough one too it commenced at sunrise and lasted till 8 ocl in the evening.

Our forces were Defeated with Severe Loss. I could not give any idea of our Losses without Describeing the Battle ground. as we. as yet have had no official report. It was in the worst place that we could have been Placed in for a general Battle. In what is termed Piney Woods, near Sabine Cross Roads. We Had Driven the enemy 8. or 10. miles During the early part of the Day until we arrived at the opening across which they retreated and our army at about 3 P.M. advanced across and commenced the fight again but the Rebels. As they always Do at the right time. Received reinforcements and the fight now became one of the most Desperate and Bloody Conflicts that has occurred during the War. At about 6 p.m. our shattered Regts were obliged to retreat across the opening or field and after fighting so long were out of ammunition. It was at this moment that the Rebels made a charge along the whole line they came out of the woods like Howling Demons. Our Artilery fairly mowed them Down by Hundreds. But nothing would stop them when they saw that our line was Broken. The whole 19th Army Corps was within a few miles of us and were now coming to our support but with just 20 minutes to late to save the Battle. The rebels Drove us Back about three miles. When the 19th Corps came up and formed line of Battle and when the Rebs came Down on them they found a warm reception. And was obliged to Halt and retreat themselves. It was however only to get out of range of our rifles for it was now 9 p.m. and quite dark and impossible for our Army to regain their lost ground the road was so full of teems that it was impossible to Do anything to Save even our wounded that were in the hospital. An ambulances on the road it was owing to these teems that We lost 18 pieces of artillery, and our Brigade the 4th Cavalry lost every teem together with Books and Papers ammunition and all and God knows how much other Brigades lost for I have no means of finding out. But one thing is quite certain—they captured or Burned every thing on the Road for at Least two miles from the Battle ground. Where the 19th Corps cheked them the retreat continued all night as far as Pleasant Hill about 20 miles where the army came stragling in all night. The 19th army Corps after Holding the rebs in check until all that was Possible was Brought or fell Back at 2 P.M. and lasted Several hours. And resulted in the Defeat of the Rebel Army. With terrible Loss of Leife. Soldiers say who help Bury the Dead that a Person might for half a mile on one Part of this line walk on Dead Bodies and not touch the ground. It is now tattoo and I will wait till tomorrow and finish my letter so Good Night.
Claude Goings

The next day, Claude finished his letter and closing remarks:

> *Our army was so much cut up by the first Day fight that it was obliged to retreat to this Place under cover of the gunboats. We have a fight with their Pickets every Day. and expect their army will attack us Here soon. This morning at 4 ocl. We were turned out Sadled our Horses and Prepared for action. After waiting till 10 ocl we are sent to our quarters. But our Pickets are at this moment fireing and I suppose we shall soon be turned out again. So I will make Hast and finish this letter.*
> *Claude*

Eleventh New Hampshire Volunteer Regiment

Another New Hampshire soldier, Corporal Alvin Williams of the Eleventh New Hampshire Volunteer Regiment, was instantly killed at Spotsylvania, and his company commander wrote his father in New London, New Hampshire, on June 4, 1864:

> *Mr. Williams, dear Sir:*
> *Your son Alvin B. Williams, was killed by a musket ball striking him in the upper lip and killing him instantly. He had just shot at a rebel color bearer and probably hit him as he was seen to fall. It was on the 12th day of May near Spotsylvania Court House, Virginia. We buried him as well as we could and marked his grave near the place where he fell. He was a good and brave soldier and we all morning his loss and extend our sympathy to you in your affliction by the loss of your good sons in the service of their country.*
> *Yours respectfully,*
> *H.K. Little, Lt. Com'd, Co.*

Twelfth New Hampshire Volunteer Regiment

The Twelfth New Hampshire Regiment set up its camp at Arlington, Virginia, on September 27, 1862. From there, the regiment went to within a short distance of Harpers Ferry to join the Army of the Potomac in its march to Falmouth Heights opposite Fredericksburg on the Rappahannock River.

Charge of Fredericksburg, November 9, 1862.

It was on this march that Corporal Olaf L. Jewett, Company E, Twelfth New Hampshire Regiment, wrote from Orleans, Virginia, on November 9, 1862:

> *The rebs retreat as fast as we advance. I have not been sick and hope I shant for it is a bad place to be sick here. They take most everything as they pass along cattel and anything. They do not allow it but the boys will go and get what they want and run the risk of getting punished. It snowed last Friday. Our company was on picket that night and it was rather hard. I shall be glad when this war is over with so I can come home once more if I am lucky enough to come out of it all right which I think I shall.*

Corporal Jewett was killed at Chancellorsville on May 3, 1863.

Many of those who showed the white feather apparently felt little shame. One soldier in the Twelfth New Hampshire Regiment related the following incident from his own experience at Fredericksburg:

Regimental Battles

In the charge I saw one soldier falter repeatedly, bowing as if before a hurricane. He would gather himself together, gain his place in the ranks, and again drop behind. Once or twice he fell to his knees, and at last sank to the ground, still gripping his musket and bowing his head. I lifted him to his feet and said "Coward!"...His pale distorted face flamed. He flung at me, "You lie!" Yet he didn't move; he couldn't his legs would not obey him. I left him there in the mud. Soon after the battle he came to me with tears in his eyes and said, "Adjutant, pardon me, I couldn't go on, but I'm not a coward." Pardon him! I asked his forgiveness.

The Second, Fifth and Twelfth New Hampshire Volunteer Regiments participated in the mud march on January 20–23, 1863. Private Martin Haynes wrote from Falmouth on January 24, 1863:

Our division left camp Tuesday noon in a pouring rain and accomplished about a mile and a half under difficulties. Wednesday we tried again and managed about six miles. The mud was simply awful, and it was almost an utter impossibility to move the wagons and artillery at all. The Manchester Battery [New Hampshire Light Battery] was straddled along the road, a gun here and a caisson there over a stretch of three miles. And that was the way everything on wheels was hold up. Yesterday the Division made its way back to the old camp.

Sixteenth New Hampshire Volunteer Regiment

William Steele of the Sixteenth New Hampshire Volunteer Regiment, writing from Carrollton, Louisiana, on March 3, 1863, said: "we don't see enny sines of having enny fiting to do and I gess we shant have enny if wee stay hear till our time is out I don't warnt to see enyy my selph. If we can git along withouth it but we have some very brave men here that want to see some and I think they would be the first man than would run."

On March 12, 1863, Steele wrote:

Dear Wife
We have moved up the river about one hundred And forty miles. Batton rouge is the capital of LA we are about sixteen miles from fort hutson. That is pretty strongly fortfid by the rebels. We have A very large force.

At this place some set the Armmy As large as sixty thousand. We had A grand revue here today. it was about four miles from our incampment. Our brigade [First Brigade, Third Division] *is on holes plantain about to miles from the sitty we have for regiments in our brigade. Whare we had the revue was at camp banks where the battle was fort last summer when batten rouge was taken from the rebels. It looks a little as tho we mint see some fun before a grate while. If the rebels don't leave fort hutson but I don't think the sixteenth will see fort hutson till the fiting is all over with. Our brigade is gnto to be held in resurve to hold the weekist plase. I don't expect to go with the regiment when it moves to help A Tac fort hutson. The dr. saz that I must stay to help gard our baggage. Thare will be A hundred men left to gard our camp grond as we have not been orded to strike our tents, our army will move before meney days to take fort hutson I expect and thay will take it without A bout. The gun bots will do most of the fitting and the land forcies will cut thire retreat. Think we shall be At home by the middle of July. Some think by the fifteenth of June. It don't so much like moving as it did when I ben to rite. We have had order to level our parade grond whare we pitched tents it was pretty ruf. If we was gon to leave in A few days we probley would not had orders to leveled our pradeground but we have difrent orders every little while. Some think that we shall be held in rezeve to gard this plase. Thare has got to be A large force left hear to hold this place in cace our troops git defeted at fort hutson but thine is no chance for the rebels to git Away from hutson unless thay make A move shortley for thay are hemde in on most every side. I gess you hear all cind of fruitful things About our Armmey in west. The big men hear think that fort Hutson and vixksburg is about the same as taken now. It is reported that our fleet has past vixksburg and now is beetenen thare And for hutson and we are be loe them.*

Eighteenth New Hampshire Volunteer Regiment

According to historian Mather Cleveland, the following account is given by an unknown soldier of the Eighteenth Regiment:

Over eighty-five per cent of the 978 volunteers recruited for the 18th Regiment were native of New Hampshire. One hundred and eighty-eight, including most of the officers, had served previously in other New

Hampshire Regiments. Slightly over seventy-five per cent of them enlisted for one year and the remainder for three years of service. Each received a Federal bounty of thirty-three dollars and a State bounty of $100.

The original five Companies of this Regiment, a little later joined by the 6th Company at City Point, Virginia, were designated the 18th New Hampshire Battalion under the command of Lieut. Colonel Joseph M. Clough who mustered in October 18, 1864.

On November 8, 1864, the Battalion cast 233 votes for President Lincoln and seventy-two for General McClellan. In December the 18th New Hampshire Battalion moved briefly into the intrenchments before Petersburg with General Benham's command to support the IX Army Corps.

On January 27, 1865, Lieutenant Colonel Joseph M. Clough wrote from City Point, Virginia:

Headquarter 18th N.H.V.
It has been cold and ice in the river so that boats have been delayed…I have been out today with my command to see deserter hung by the neck until he was dead, dead, dead. He was hung near my camp. All the troops were formed in a square and open ranks. At 12 o'clock the culprit was marched through under guard, band playing the dirge on each side of the culprit marched a chaplin, his arms were tied behind him. He looked careworn and pale but took a firm step arriving in front of the gallows prayers were offered after which he was blindfolded the rope was put around his neck the platform let down and he was launched into eternity after which the troops marched around to take a lost loo at the fate of a deserter.

I am having company most every day. Fuller is with me of the 4th in charge of Colonel Bells things. Colonel Bell has been sent home. [Colonel Louis Bell, Fourth New Hampshire Regiment, was killed at Fort Fisher, North Carolina, on January 15, 1865.] *We had a little fun the other night. Three rebel rams came down the James River to make a dash on this point thinking our Monitors were all gone but they got a warm reception. One of them was blown up by our batteries, and the other two got back as soon as possible. They probably wont try that game again soon. Yours*

J.M. Clough, Lieut. Col. Comd.

New Hampshire Cavalry Battalion, First New England Cavalry

The cavalry, under Major General George Stoneman, was forming a screen for the infantry marching toward Falmouth. Private Austin Whipple wrote the following on November 8, 1862, from Waterloo, Virginia: "The N.H. 10th came into this place last night, no one in it I know. The N.H. 6th, 9th, 11, & 12th they say are about two miles from us. I hope we shall pass them or they us. Tell mother I want her to be preparing me a flannel shirt and drawers, some feetings and mittings with a forefinger."

Another of Whipple's letters, dated December 4, 1862, reads as follows:

Camp at Gen. Whipple's Hq.—2 or 3 miles from Falmoth.

My horse got the "mud foot rot." I was given another and went to General Robinsons. He has command of the brigade under General Birney. The Brigade lay near the N.H. 11th, 9th, and 6th and I saw boy from the 11th several times, also the N.H. 2nd, 5th, & 12th are near here and we see men from them often. I am an orderly for Gen. Whipple. [Brigadier General Amiel Whipple, commanding the Third Division, III Army Corps; Brigadiar General John C. Robinson, commanding First Brigade, First Division, II Army Corps]

Confederate assault on the works near Washington repulsed by dismounted cavalry and militia, July 12, 1864.

Regimental Battles

First New Hampshire Volunteer Artillery Regiment

The first major engagement of this battery occurred on August 29, 1862, at Groveton, Virginia, where the Second Regiment took part in the assault on Stonewall Jackson's Confederate Corps; the battery lost.

At four o'clock in the morning on September 17, 1861, an aide rode into the battery at Antietam and told the battery commander:

> *Come into battery one hundred yards to the front loaded with canisters and when you hear the report of my pistol commence firing as rapidly as you please. In a ravine of the opposite side of the road is a whole division of the enemy buried in deep sleep.*
>
> *We did as ordered and the muzzles of six twelve-pound howitzers were aimed directly into the mass of sleeping humanity. It seemed cruel, but when is war anything else? The expected signal came and in an instant the lanyards were pulled. The opposite side of the ravine was quickly changed into a howly, writhing mass of astonished Johnnies. The destruction must have been fearful though we did not have an opportunity to examine that part of the field afterward. We were of course answered by their batteries and in a very few minutes the road of battle reached the whole length of our lines, our position being on the extreme right.*

On that same morning, we have a description of the second position of the battery where it relieved the Massachusetts Battery, which was badly shot up. The account continues:

> *Not ten yards in front of where this battery has stood was a rail fence, and behind that the rebels had marched up their line of battle many times, for their dead actually lay corded up behind that fence to such a degree, that when we were ordered to pass through we tore down the fence and had to move away many dead bodies before the horses could be made to go through for they will never step upon a man's body, if they find room for their feet.*

First New Hampshire Volunteer Sharpshooters Regiment

On December 22, 1861, in a letter from the camp of instruction for United States sharpshooters, Lieutenant Ben Calef, quartermaster, First New Hampshire Volunteer Sharpshooters Regiment, wrote:

We have moved our abode this last week to our own camp on the hill opposite the first Reg't...I was quite amused as well as pleased to hear from Dr. Hale of the 2ⁿᵈ Reg't of a kind conspiracy to get me into the 2ⁿᵈ their headquarters being found incompetive. The Dr. and Col. Post of the 2ⁿᵈ were at the house the other evening and they with Mrs. Berdan made an attack on the Col. [Berdan]. The Col. Insisted on my staying as he depended entirely upon me to it etc...I wish to be with you Christmas... New companies may be arriving that will give us something to attend to.

On November 22, 1862, the First and Second United States Sharpshooters were stationed at Fredericksburg and Falmouth. Lieutenant Calef wrote: "Our Reg't was sent out on picket for two days. Today our Division moves to Brook Station about four miles from here on the Aquia Creek and Fredericksburg R.R. Col. Post has not returned from his last trip to Washington. I wish he would return with what he deserves, a star on his shoulders."

On January 18, 1863, from the headquarters of sharpshooters, Lieutenant Calef wrote:

Col. Berdan now commands all the Sharpshooters in the Army of the Potomac and they are divided among those grand divisions. The 2ⁿᵈ Reg't has gone back with the Left; five companies of the 1ˢᵗ are with the Right; the other five companies remain with the Center. I am relieved from duty with the Second Reg't and am chief Q.M. [quartermaster] of Sharpshooters. We move our quarters over to Gen'l Burnside.

On June 24, 1863, from "Camp near Gum Springs, Virginia," Lieutenant Ben Calef wrote:

We are in a state of glorious uncertainty. It is the meanest campaign we have ever had. Our Corps is acting in the reserve. It is all suspense, falling in, marching, halting, dependent entirely upon the movement of the advance. The general opinion seem to be first that there will be no fight, save perhaps a scrimmage—that the rebels having by a small force up this way and that Gen'l Hooker is decidedly puzzled as to what they are doing...Col. Berdan now commands the largest Brigade in the Army, over twenty-two hundred men as large as our old Division...We have had on this trip long and tedious marches, the dust has been fearful, the living miserable. Mrs. Berdan presented the Colonel with a new recruit the other day, a little girl, "Mother and child are doing well."

Regimental Battles

THE SHARPSHOOTERS AT GETTYSBURG

On July 2, 1863, while the sharpshooters were heavily engaged at Gettysburg, from near Westminster, Maryland, some twenty miles away, Quartermaster Lieutenant Calef wrote:

> *We arrived here with our train the forenoon after a pull of thirty-six miles, without halting save to find the animals. Our troops left us Tuesday [June 30] and I judge now from the very heavy firing that a large battle is going on. They spread the tale yesterday that Gen'l Reynolds was killed, our old Corps commander when we were in the 1ˢᵗ Corps. Well, Gen'l Hooker is out as I predicted he would be…have nothing to say about his successor, the junior Major-General almost in the Army. I hope not one of the wretches will escape home. We have a thousand of them penned up here in town that we took yesterday…I just heard from the command that they are at Gettysburg in Pennsylvania. We may get into Mass. Yet. We are in a civilized country now.*

The position held, and the action engaged in by the sharpshooters at Gettysburg was described in Colonel Berdan's official report, submitted on July 29, 1863. It reads, in part:

> *Early on the morning of July second, I posted the Second Regiment, Major Stoughton commanding, on our left to act as flankers and the First Regiment on our front. About 7:30 A.M. I received orders to send forward a detachment of 100 sharpshooters to discover if possible what the enemy was doing. I went with the detail and posted them on the hill beyond on the Emmitsburg Road, where they kept up a constant fire upon the enemy in the woods beyond until they were driven in about 5 P.M. by a heavy force of the enemy after having expanding all their units. About 11 A.M. I received an order from Major General Birney to send out another detachment of 100 Sharpshooters farther to the left of our line and to take the Third Maine Volunteer as support, with instructions to find the enemy and discover their movement. I moved down the Emmitsburg Road some distance beyond our extreme left and deployed the Sharpshooters.*
> *…We soon came upon the enemy and drove them sufficiently to discover three columns in motion in the rear of the woods…We attacked them vigorously on the flank…We were enabled to do great execution and threw them for a time into confusion. They soon rallied, however, and attacked*

A sharpshooter from Berdan's Riflemen, First Regiment, Company C, takes aim in battle.

The Battle of Gettysburg, July 1–3, 1863.

us when having accomplished the object of the reconnaissance. I withdrew under cover of the woods, bringing off most of our wounded and reported about 2 o'clock to Major Birney.

The Second Regiment was deployed in front of the Second Brigade by order of General Ward and moved forward to a favorable position where they had the enemy's skirmishers in check and did good execution, breaking the enemy's front line three times and finally fell back as the enemy advanced in heavy force. The balance of the First Regiment under immediate command of Captain Baker moved forward to the right of the Peach Orchard, on the right of the First Brigade, where they had a splendid chance for execution, the enemy coming forward in heavy lines.

On the 3rd a detachment of 100 Sharpshooters was sent under Captain Baker to cover the front of the Sixth Corps…I desire to make special mention of Colonel Lakeman and Major Lee of the Third Maine Regiment for their services on reconnaissance. We went into action with about 450 rifles. During three days we expanded 14,400 rounds of ammunition. Our total loss was 12 killed, 59 wounded, and 18 missing.

The Opening Battle between the USS *Kearsarge* and the CSS *Alabama*, June 19, 1864

For one year, Captain John A. Winslow of the USS *Kearsarge* chased after Confederate ship CSS *Alabama*, and when he learned that the Rebel ship was laying at the harbor in Cherbourg, France, seeking repairs, Captain Winslow headed his ship off in pursuit.

"The contest will no doubt be contested and obstinate, but the two war ships are so equally matched that I do not feel at liberty to decline it," remarked Captain Semmes of the *Alabama* when the *Kearsarge* came within sight.

An unknown New Hampshire seaman described the battle that day:

Balls rolled in at the portholes and swept away the gunners of the CSS Alabama, and several pierces of the hull below the waterline, making the ship tremble from stem to stern, thus letting in the flood of water. The vessel had described seven circles, and the Alabama's deck was strewn with the dead when, at the end of the hour, the boat was found to be sinking, and the officers, with a keen sense of chivalry threw into the sea their swords that were no longer their own.

The *Deerhound* rescues Captain Semmes.

Opening of the fight between the USS *Kearsarge* and the CSS *Alabama*, June 19, 1864.

The boat the *Deerhound* rescued Captain Semmes. At 12:24 p.m., Captain Semmes from the CSS *Alabama* struck his colors after ninety minutes of battle with the USS *Kearsarge*; the *Alabama* was seen disappearing beneath the sea.

Semmes, in his official notes, indicated the following:

> *At the end of the engagement, it was discovered, by those of our officers who went alongside the enemy's ship with the wounded, that her midship section on both sides was thoroughly iron-coated. The planking had been ripped off in every direction by our shot and shells and the chain broken and indented in many places, and forced partly into the ship's side. The enemy was heavier than myself, both in ship, battery, and crew, but I did not know until action was over that she was also iron-clad.*

Chapter 4
Health and Welfare

THE SICK IN HOSPITAL

"It scares a man to death to get sick down here," wrote one soldier from New England. Indeed, during the war, more men died from disease than from bullets. By 1862, there were 131 officially sanctioned medical centers available, the most ever to that date. Each brigade surgeon relied heavily on such items as Epsom salts, opium and whiskey, which were considered cure-alls. Turpentine was sometimes used to treat diarrhea; chloroform and ether were used as anesthetics; and a liberal dose of morphine dulled the pain of dressed wounds and amputated limbs.

Typical of the early institutions was the Alexandria Hospital, in which the wounded from battles such as First Manassas were treated. It was located in an old seminary and may be described as follows:

July 1861
It is an irregular structure, and badly adapted to hospital purposes. Its halls and stairways are narrow and adapt, and many of its wards small and difficult of access. Its immediate precincts are damp…and the wood-work of its piazzas and sheds is rapidly decaying. Ventilation is even now very defective and an unhealthy odor pervades the building. The latter is due in measure to the fact that troops recently quartered in the building, had been allowed to accumulate filth in some of the upper rooms and the cellar…There being no-indoor water-closets or baths, the same necessary for conveying close-stools through the house induces the risk that obtains

in the Union Hotel and other Hospitals...There is no dead-house. This hospital now contains ninety-six patients.

According to *Medical and Surgical History*, vol. 3, the medical service in the battlefields consisted of the following:

> *The personnel of the division hospital consisted of a surgeon in charge, with an Assistant Surgeon as executive officer and a second Assistant Surgeon as recorder, an operating staff of three Surgeons aided by three Assistant Surgeons, and the requisite number of nurses and attendants.*
>
> *The division ambulance train was commanded by First Lieutenant of the line, assisted by a Second Lieutenant for each brigade. The enlisted men detailed for ambulance duty were a sergeant for each regiment, three privates for each ambulance, and one private for each wagon. The ambulance train consisted of from one to three ambulances for each regiment, squadron, or battery, a medicine wagon for each brigade, and two or more supply wagons. The hospital and ambulance train were under the control of the Surgeon-in-chief of the Division. The division hospitals were usually located just out of range of artillery fire. Sometimes three or more division hospitals were consolidated under the orders of a Corps Medical Commissary, and chief ambulance officer.*

Medical wagons contained field first-aid kits. The cowhide (which cost the government $110 each) contained fifty-two medicines, plus such items as condensed milk, sponges, tourniquets, candles and silk for sewing wounds.

A diary of a Union officer describes the following conditions of the field hospital:

> *Tuesday, May 10th, 1864*
> *Ambulances and army wagons with two tiers of flooring, loaded with wounded and drawn by four and six mule teams, pass along the plank corduroy road to Fredericksburg...*
>
> *Under three large "tent flies," the center which was one that largest of all, stood three heavy wooden tables, around which were grouped a number of surgeons and their assistants. They were bareheaded and clad in long linen dusters reaching nearly to the ground, which were covered with blood from top to bottom and had the arms cut off or roll up to the shoulders. The stretcher-bearer deposited their ghastly freight side by side in a windrow on the ground in front of the table under the first tent fly. Here a number of*

assistants took charge of the poor fellows, and as some of them lifted a man onto the first table others moved up the windrow so that no time nor space should be lost.

The medical officers not employed at the field hospitals accompanied their regiments and established temporary depots as near as practicable to the line of battle.

As soon as possible after every engagement the wounded were transferred from the division or corps hospitals to the base or general hospitals.

Corporal Claude Goings wrote this letter while convalescing from his second illness at Camp Kearney, Louisiana, on October 25, 1862:

The hospital is full as they can crowd it all the time the fever and ague is terrible for soldiers here now there is 25 in tents and 9 in the hospital, members of our company and ours is better of than some others so you can judge by that how many is sick in the Regt...I am gaining my strength a little but I don't think I shall get well enough to Drill or do guard Duty again while I am here but if they die as fast as they did up to Camp Parapet it will take me half the time to Paint the Broads [wooden markers for the graves of dead soldiers].

James B. Wiggin wrote this letter to his family in Tamworth, New Hampshire:

Newport Va. August 24 the '62.
Dear Brother & Sister
It is with pleasure I write to you to day. I received your letter and my box yesterday. Oh! Holy moses wasn't tickled to death. The first thing I done was got drunk. Well I never was so much pleased before every thing was all wright as an old irish woman used to say to me may god be with you.

Our army has all left the perninsular we expect to go up with pope there is going to be some more har fighting. I do not want to see any more for one. I am here at Newport news the doctor sent me here to recruit up. I shall not be with the regiment again until I get better than I have been since our retreat that was the hardest thing. I do no duty since I have gut the rheumatism so I have to walk with crutches. I am very well other wise this is a good healthy place here is about 2,000 sick and disabled soldiers here now lame and crippled in all shapes they don't die off very fast.

Thank God we have gut off the battle ground for a spell we have all seen some hard times you can't go in a place on the perninsular but what it stinks with dead soldiers not half buried. But our army is now agoing to try another area to attack Richmond. I don't see any signs of the war ever ending. I am sorry that Isaiah is or have been very sick. I have never heard from him only by way of you. Funy I have never hurd from simon he left where do you suppose he is. I have not heard from Tamworth for 3 months. I suppose mary has steped out on me if she has she can kiss my ass. Don't let any one know about it. She gets mad just because I don't write every week. I can't get paper not find time to write as I used to in muddy branch. I did not have any paper now so I rote on your letter. Sarah, I am agoing to have my minature taken which I am here for there is a chance and I may not have a chance again by mail. You will say you have gut a hard looking brother for I am black as a crow and rather poor. Hannah then is up home enjoying all the comforts of life. Willard are you going to enlist or be drafted. Now Sarah you said you would write me a good long letter when I get my things now I have them and have rote you a long letter now answer both you and Will. And Foly tell Foly them cakes was very nice. I ate them like a pig no like a hog. If you should write up home tell them I am well and ready to die for my country. I shall have to close for the paper is most full direct your letters to Newport News.

I don't know how long I shall stay here in the hospital but I think I shall not be fit for fighting for some time. Give my love to all.
Yours,
James B. Wiggin

This note of appreciation and love was sent to his sister from the Wolf Street Hospital in August 1862:

Dear Sister Sarah,
I need a letter from you with $7.00 enclosed. I was glad to hear from you and to receive the money for we live dreadful poor here in the hospittle. I tell you Sarah I never knew what it was to be sick before. I have had the thypoid fever 5 weeks lord sake you ought to see my hands and legs. I don't weight over 90 pounds. I have not set up any till last Friday. I was out of my hear 4 days all of the time but I am getting along first rate.

They say that I am going to have a discharge and if I do I shall come home in about 2 weeks. Sarah when I get paid off again I shall have $52.00 and if I get discharged I shall get 100 Dollars Bounty and then

I can go home quite merry. I tell you Sarah we have hard living here it is nothing but hay tea & dry Bread. The Dr. is giving me something now that is nourishing. He gives me one boiled egg a day and toast and sweetens my tea. Sarah, I must close and go to bed or I shall be sick to morrow. Direct your letter J.B.W., Wolf St. Hospittle, Alexandria, Va.

p.s. Give my love to all the folks and a share for your self. Sarah I am obliged to you for your kindness. You are the best sister I have got for waiting on me and if I ever get able I shall remember it. Good By.

Your loving brother

This unsigned note of concern was sent from the New Hampshire Cavalry Battalion camp near Falmouth on December 17, 1862:

Mr. Russell
Dear Sir.
It is with sadness that I sit down to inform you that Austin L. Whipple is a prisoner. He was taken at the battle of Fredericksburg and is paroled I think. When you hear from him please let me now for I feel anxious.

On January 12, 1863, on his arrival at the United States General Hospital in Maryland, Austin Whipple dictated to a friend the following letter:

On Sunday A.M. at 5 o'clock Dec. 14th I went out with Lieut. Eddy, one of Gen' Whipple's staff officers and by a misunderstanding on his part we rode into the Rebel lines and were taken prisoner. I was marched to Richmond, which fatigued me very much and I caught cold at night. I arrived at Libby Prison the next Wednesday and in two days was taken sick and in a short time I was unable to help myself. The physician paid me no attention and I had to lay upon the filthy floor. I was soon covered with lice but some fellows in the 25th N. Jersey took as good care of me as they could which without doubt saved my life. I left Richard on the 10th inst. And arrived here today. I was washed and clean clothes put on me and I am now in a good soft bed. My lungs are much affected and I have a very bad cough. The surgeon gave me some medicine am now very weak and the prospect looks dark. I think I shall have the best of care. This is a first rate Hospital.

On January 23, 1863, Mrs. Leverett wrote to Mrs. Whipple the following: "It now becomes my painful duty to inform you he is dead. After death he looked as calm and peaceful as if in sleep. He will be buried in the soldiers burying ground about mile from town."

On July 12, 1863, Corporal Goings again wrote from the hospital in New Orleans:

> *The report is that our Regt is going Home to recruit. I hope it will as there is not one Hundred men fit for duty. We have at last got the old Miss River Cleaned out and guess we shall keep it this time. If they would do as well in Virginia as we have here the war would soon close. There is over one hundred of the 16th Regt. Here. I was very glad to hear Charley Pike had got out of the war safe Home. Tell him to make that old Rebel fiddle ring for Vicksburg and Port Hudson.*

While stationed in Algiers, Louisiana, Private William Steele wrote on May 12, 1863, of a visit to Barracks Hospital to visit some sick soldiers in Company G, Sixteenth Regiment:

> *Sunday May 1863*
> *I got a pass to go to the sitty and visit some of our sick boys. I started a bout eight P.M. I took along with me A jar of black current jel for Walter Chamblin* [Private Walter Chamberlin] *I took the horse carse to visit the United States barracks some five miles from orlens. We rode a bout four miles threw the sitty then we come to A farming community. I got to the Barricks a bout leven oclock the first one I enquired for was Walter. The ancer was he is ded and bured. That was hard news for me I can tell you but the por boy has gon to his long restingplase and where no traveler returnes. It will be hard new for his folks but that* [they ain't] *along in there trubel. There was a boy by the name of felch* [Private George W. Felch] *that belong to our company from Ware NH in the same barracks that dide a few days before Walter did. I saw our captain about ten days before Walter dide And he thought he would git well. I made all the inquire I could in regard to the treatment he had. I cold find no one but sed he had the best of care. Our Col and Sun* [Colonel James F. Pike and his son, Private James T. Pike, Company E] *was present when he dide and went to the grave when he was buried. Not menney col would do that I can assure you. I did not go to Walters grave but I shall gorge ramond* [Private George B. Ramond] *told me that the word master had ritter to mr chimblings folks the holl particular in regard to walters deth. The gar of gel that I spoke of that I was taking Along to Walter I gave to one of our Lyndbrow boys. There is*

nine men in the barracks that belong to our company. three is from lyndebrow
Hames Boutwell [Private James Boutwell died at home on August
15, 1863] *george ramond mikel ford* [Private Michael Ford] *John*
Carken [Private John C. Carkin] *is in the university hospital in the sitty.*
Abrim Boutwell [Private Abram Boutwell] *is in the charity Hospital.*
They all seame to be gitting Along niseley.

Private Steele was writing only about comrades in Company G of the
Sixteenth New Hampshire Volunteer Regiment and in particular those from
Lyndeborough, New Hampshire, or the vicinity.

During the later half of 1863, the Third, Fourth and Seventh Volunteer
Regiments remained in South Carolina on Morris Island. On November 8,
1863, Captain J.M. Clough, Company H, Fourth Regiment, wrote:

I have had company for three days. some hospital matrons from the army
of the Potomack one a Mrs. Marden a widow lady about fifty years
of age formerly of Windham, N.H. and has a son in this regiment
[Private Lemuel Marden, Company K, Fourth Regiment, from
Windham, served three years]. *She had bin on the battlefield of*
Antiteham and Getesburg and late from the hospital at Getisburg. She is now
sent to this department and assigned in the hospitals at Beauford come up
to see her son. The other is a maiden lady about forty by the name of Miss
Dame [Harriet Patience Dame] *from Concord. She was with the N.H.*
2nd two years and has bin all through the penensuliah campaign and at the
Battle of Getisburg but of late at the New England rooms in Washington.
her object is to visit the N.H. Regiments and see how the hospitals look and
what can be sent to them to make them comfortable that are sick outside of
this Sanitary Commishion or what is called the Christian Commishion.
The Sanitary has done some good but this Christian Commishion is a
complete humbug and in some cases the Sanitary has bin for the good things
never reached the sick but was gobbled up by officers and Docts for their
own use. Miss Dame is surprised that the people of N.H. have never took
any interest in the regiments here that they have at other places. I told her
we had got along thus far and I guess we could stand it through I gave them
my tents and beds. I also set them to my table, which I know is the best.
They have bin with me three nights but tonight they have gone to the 3rd
N.H. I have had a pleasant visit with them. Yesterday visit Wagner now
Fort Strong also Gregg not Fort Putnam the enemy war firing briskly but
they showed they had seen shell but not quite as big as here.

Health and Welfare

On July 31, 1864, Captain J.M. Clough dictated a letter from the XVIII Army Corps Hospital as follows:

I was wounded yesterday morning, the 30th, a ball passing through my right hand thus I am disabled from writing so Willie is writing for me. There is a probability of loosing my thumb but I am in hopes to save it. I was wounded while leading my regiment on a charge. I came out of the fight before it terminated therefore I am unable to tell the result. Our loss is very heavy in our regiment. Lieut. Adams is with me wounded the ball passing through his leg above the knee [Second Lieutenant Mathew Adams, Company H, Fourth New Hampshire, later captain of Company A].

The Fifth New Hampshire Volunteer Regiment was the next in action on June 16, 17 and 18, 1864, when sixteen of the troops were killed. On July 4, 1864, Private Daniel W. George, Company E, Fifth New Hampshire Regiment, wrote:

Camp near Petersburg, Va.
Cousin Eddy
We have some pretty tough times for the past 5 weeks. Tom Parker was killed. E. Tucker and C. Spooner was wounded out of our drum core and that is the most there is in the army out of one drum Core. I have been very lucky and thankful that I have gone through this army so well. If I get out with one arm or leg I shall think myself one of the luckiest men in the world. There is plenty of time to get my head nocked off yet. I am at the general hospital now back some four miles from the front and I don't go up there only when I am obliged to and that is not very often now. I am thinking of my liberty so you can go and come when you are a mind to. Don't you come until you are obliged to and then you had better go some place and hide yourself and not let them catch you if you want to live. You don't hear one half that are killed wounded or missing. They are a frade to let the folks now it for fear they would not fight. I have got three months and fifteen days longer to stay in the service and then I shall serve three years and that is enough for me. A man that lives through this war and gets out all safe—there is not anything that will kill him. He is bomb proof and there is not any disease that can kill him…he will live always or some time.

The Fifth Army Corps awaiting the orders to advance after the explosion of the mine in front of Petersburg, July 30, 1864.

Historian Mather Cleveland wrote in *New Hampshire Fights the Civil War*:

The Mississippi Campaign cost the IX Corps very few battle casualties but a great many of these New Hampshire troops died of disease or were hospitalized for illness. Typhoid, dysentery and malaria took a fearful toll of these soldiers. Of their return trip up the Mississippi River, Private George Morgan, Company F 11th New Hampshire, wrote on August 18. 1863, "John Saunder's of our Co. died of swamp fever the morning we gut to Memphis and Charles Colby died to Covington, our drummer. Walt Pingerey and Ben Sargent ant much better than dead. They left Ben Sargent to Memphis where he died."

Major General Simon Goodell Griffin wrote of this Mississippi Campaign:

It was the most disastrous campaign to the health, strength, numbers, and morale of our men that we ever experienced. They were attacked with fever, congestive chills, chronic diarrhoea and kindred disease. Many died, others were ruined in health and constitution. The sickness on the boats was terrible and almost universal. Every night as we lay up on account of low water, there was a burial party ashore.

Health and Welfare

On December 13, 1862, Private Albert M. Putnam, Company I, Thirteenth Volunteer Regiment, whose military service tended as an ambulance driver, wrote:

Camp near Fredericksburg.
For the last month I have had to drive in the amblance 100 wounded sick
& ded men. This has ben the hardest battle since the wair began. It was
hard to sea the men cut to peaces.

On January 1, 1863, Private Putnam continued:

You wanted to now if I had seen a rebel. I have sen a large number of them.
I sea their camp and thair camps is not more than 1½ miles from hear. I
will tell you that the battle that we had hear was the hardest wone that has
ben fort since the rebelon began. I have sen the horrows of a hard fort battle
and a man can not tell what he can stand till he has tried it.

The Thirteenth Volunteer Regiment records the following account by Assistant Surgeon John Sullivan to illustrate the intensity of rifle fire and the danger from this even in the rear:

I was loading my ambulance one day at Cold Harbor with wounded men
to send to the Corps Hospital when a bullet struck the near horse just back
of the shoulder and passed through the horse, which instantly fell dead, then
entered the off horse in a like manner and lodged under the skin on the off
side. This horse stood a moment and then fell dead on the near horse.

The Thirteenth Volunteer Regiment left Cold Harbor on June 12 for White House Landing and, proceeding by steamer, reached its old campground at Bermuda Hundred on June 14, 1864.

On June 23, 1864, ambulance driver Albert Putnam wrote the following from Portsmouth, Virginia:

We are taking the poor wonded men from the steam botes as thay arrive
from the battle field to the hospittle…am a havin the fever and agure…I
am well won day or towe and then I am sick…I shake and freas and then
I am on fire and my head and limes will ake a nof to make a man go wild
from 2 to 6 hours to a time…I am taking quinine and whiskey to try to
break up the agure.

Pneumonia afflicted the weak. With only tents to protect them against the cold and snow, the men faced increasing risk for disease. *Courtesy of the New Hampshire Historical Society, Concord, New Hampshire.*

From the records of the Fourteenth Volunteer Regiment, Surgeon Thayer wrote the following account on September 10, 1863, from Washington:

My hospital attendants are all of them so much worn and about sick that I sent all the sick in hospital up to the Finley Hospital last night. I shall clean up the air and let the attendants rest for a few days. An orderly came last ev'g from Dr. Baxter of the Campbell Hospital asking for two companies of men to put down a mutiny among hospital guards and men of the Invalid Corps. 200 men under Major Duncan went off on the double quick. Things had quieted down somewhat when they arrived. Very little blood had been spilled and no lives. He arrested some of the mutineers and left a guard of fifty men for the night.

On October 19, 1863, Thayer wrote of the attrition in the regiment:

The reg't is getting cleared to some extent of its least efficient officers. Three have just been discharged and some more are likely to follow. We have a very fine regiment of men and if we had all good officers no N.H. Regiment would be better…

Just a year ago yesterday we left Concord. We reported today 157 less than then. 60 of them died. The remainder have deserted or been discharged for disability or transferred to the Invalid Corps. So much loss without going under fire. Only one man has deserted in the last six months and he was arrested. The 90 recruits which started from Concord have not returned.

The Fourteenth Volunteer Regiment fought at Cedar Creek in October 1864. General Sheridan reached the field of battle at 10:30 a.m., and he found the majority of his army deployed. At 4:00 p.m., the Union troops attacked the Confederates, who in turn retreated in demoralized rout. During this action, the Fourteenth Regiment, with regained strength of three hundred, had twelve killed and about twenty-five wounded.

Surgeon Thayer of the Fourteenth Volunteer Regiment wrote of the Battle of Cedar Creek about three years after the war:

During the battle I had walked to the rear looking for a safe place for the wounded. Men were limping along around me, some leaning on comrades, some carried on stretchers. The ambulances were out of range in the rear. I looked in vain for an opportunity to take care of the wounded. One of our boys just able to walk, with a bullet in his thigh, stopped while I extracted it and set out a slow pace and with good grit for the Corps hospital three miles off. At last a quarter of a mile in the rear of the final rallying point, I found several surgeons collecting and dressing the wounded in a shelter spot from which the ambulances conveyed them to the Corps hospital at Newton. Our patients were laid on the grassy slope wounded and maimed in every way by minie balls, shells and canisters some were cold with the near approach of death. Balls were extracted, hemorrhage was checked, fractured limbs were rudely splinted to enable them to bear carriage and all were finally removed by ambulances to the hospitals. Having seen the wounded off and dined from my haversack, I turned my course toward the front—It was one o'clock.

I found my own division [Second, XIX Army Corps] *resting in line of battle with one corps* [VIII] *considerably broken—nearly a thousand of its men prisoners, three thousand killed and wounded in the 19th and 6th Corps.* [Sheridan arrived to take charge. Some historians give Major General Horatio G. Wright's VI Corps credit for saving the situation.] *To return for a moment to the rear, at the time when the afternoon advance was made we had ambulances at the edge of the woods and gave attention to the wounded as they began to come back, sending them off to Newton as soon as they could be transported. Our wounded were far less numerous than in the morning notwithstanding the impetuosity of our attack on the rebel lines. It was not long after the first onset before rebel wounded began to come to us.*

An orderly came through the wood for a surgeon for General Grover said to be dangerously wounded. I found him held upon his horse by some of his staff fortunately not dangerously wounded but faint from the shock of a shell, which tore of the breast of his coat and badly bruised his arm. His ankle had been bruised in the morning by a fall off his horse. I sent him on a stretcher to the hospital. We saw him in 3 weeks again at the head of our Division.

We continued our dressings in the rear for more than two hours until no more wounded came. It was nearly sunset. We sat down and made a comfortable supper off some corn bread from the haversack of a rebel whose mortal wounds I had dressed. My orderly had appeared at last and I was not sorry to be mounted again. Our course lay over ground with which we were not familiar but the rebel dead and other marks of battle were a sufficient guide.

I found enough to do with the poor fellows who had lain there mortally or seriously wounded since early morning. Some of the wounded had been taken up by the men and put in as comfortable quarters as could be improvised for them. Others I found where they fell and made them as easy as possible where they were till they could be removed to Newton. Hardly a man sick or well had any shelter that night. We were sobered by thoughts of the fallen and mourned for personal friends but proud of our Army and our General and grateful for our Signal Victory.

Many of our soldiers from the Union were placed in Southern prisons such as Andersonville in Georgia, where many of them lost their lives. The following is a letter of condolence:

Manchester NH July 25, 1865
Wm. B. Dodge
My Dear Sir
When I saw you last at Antrim you will remembers that I made mention of these being a mam in the 7th NH Vols who was made a prisoner on the 12th of February '64 at Fla. Since my return I have hed another conversation with this man who is a member of Co. E of that Reg't Wm Johnes by name the substence of which I will tell you. He was about one hundred others of the Reg't taken first to the Courthouse—thence to Andersonville when they arrived on the 14th of March. Johnes says that he knew Cobb well—that he was at the time of his capture acting 1st Sgt of his Co—that he was wounded and was in good & general health—As they arrived

in Andersonnville he [Cobb] was put on duty in charge of a squad of men whose duty it was to draw and isshe [issue] Rations to the men in the prison—that he sew taken sick in about one month after with severe Diachewe [diarrhea]—Mr. Johnes cannot tell definitely the time of his death but feels sure that it was in June very near the last of the month and that he was about until within a few days previous to his death. Johnes thinks that out of the 100 of his Reg't but about one tenth of them lived to be paroled. Out of four who quartered with Caleb but one lived I think his name was Kingsten of Dover.

There is a man of the same Reg't who now is a Recruiting Officer in this City who can give me the address of another who was there at Andersonnville at the same time and from the same Reg't who left a journal during his imprisonment who would be more likely able to give a more definite act as Mr Johnes says he was very fortunate to take note of all events—As I have an opportunity of seeing him I will write you again and what every I can do toward giving inteligence that will be of interest to you I will cheerfully do so.
Very Respectfully Yours,
(Kind Regards to all)
A G Bennett
(Mr. Wm B. Dodge)

ANDERSONVILLE PRISON

The following are excerpts from the diary of a Union prisoner at Andersonville from March 14, 1864, to September 8, 1864. This soldier describes some of the horrors seen and felt in the Confederate prison in Georgia:

June 18—Dying off as usual—more in number each day as the summer advances. Rebels say they don't begin to have hot weather down here until about August. Well, it is plain to me that all will die. Old prisoners have stood as long as they can, and are dropping off fast, while the new ones go anyhow. Someone stole my cap during the night. A dead neighbor furnished me another however.
July 12—All day and up at four o'clock P.M., the dead are being gathered up and carried to the south gate and placed in a row inside the dead line.

The prison camp at Andersonville, Georgia.

As the bodies are stripped of their clothing in most cases as soon as the breath leaves, and in some cases before, the row of dead presents a sickening appearance. Leg drawn up and in all shapes. They are black from pitch pine smoke and laying in the sun. Some of them lay there for twenty hours or more, and by that time are in horrible condition. At four o'clock a four or six mule wagon comes up to the gate and twenty or thirty bodies are loaded onto the wagon and they are carried off to be put in trenches, one hundred in each trench, in the cemetery, which is eighty or a hundred rods away.

May 19—Nearly twenty thousand men confined here now. New ones coming every day. Rations very small and very poor. The meal that the bread is made out of is ground, seemingly, cob and all, and it scourges the men fearfully. Things getting continually worse. Hundreds of cases of dropsy. Men puff out of human shape and are perfectly horrible to look at.

Union medical corps records of surgeon casualties indicate the extent of the doctors' dedication and the risks they took to help their men: surgeons killed in battle numbered 42, with 83 wounded, while another 290 Union surgeons died of disease or in accidents.

Health and Welfare

LOSSES OF NEW HAMPSHIRE REGIMENTS

Historian Hobart Pillsbury relates the following account in his *New Hampshire in the Civil War*:

> *The Fifth Regiment lost the greatest number of men killed, though the Twelfth suffered most heavily in proportion to its numbers, losing over one-tenth of its members on the field, while the loss of the Fifth was less than one-twelfth. The 1ˢᵗ Sixteenth and Seventeenth Regiments lost no men killed in battle. The Ninth lost the greatest absolute number, but the Sixteenth the greatest percentage by disease. The deaths in the later amounted to over 20 per cent, notwithstanding it was never in an engagement. The number of desertions varied with the number and character of the recruits received in the latter months of war. Many deserted on their way to the field and never reached the regiment to which they were assigned.*
>
> *The authorities of the State looked well to the needs of her soldiers under all circumstances. Colonel Frank E. Howe, of the city of New York, and Robert R. Carson, of Philadelphia, were early appointed agents to look after, provide and care for the sick and wounded soldiers of New Hampshire who were in hospitals or passing through these cities, and each forwarded monthly reports of names, disability and deaths in the several hospitals, and other important facts in relation to soldiers coming under their observation. Other agents were appointed and sent to army hospitals and battlefields to look after the sick and wounded and bury the dead.*

Chapter 5
Diary of Freedom Sanborn

From the archive of the Sanbornton historical records, the following account is given:

> *On August 12, 1862, Freedom Sanborn enlisted in the 12th New Hampshire Regiment, fought in the battle of Fredericksburg, Chancellorsville, and was wounded at the Battle of Gettysburg on July 2, 1863. A ball passed through his throat, shattering his windpipe so as to prevent his speaking aloud for one year. As a farmer, he settled with his father at the bay. On October 1, 1873, at the age of 32, he died of a heart disease induced by his army experience.*

The following is from a diary of his experiences during the Civil War—the bloodiest war in American history:

> *It was a balmy Tuesday afternoon on August 12th when I enlisted in the Belknap County Regiment, which was stationed in Laconia, New Hampshire. I was very excited, for this was going to be most enjoyable adventure; we're goin' to beat those rebels—no question about that.*
>
> *On Monday, the 25th, our regiment went into camp at Laconia, for routine examination and drilling.*
>
> *The people of the Carroll and Belknap Counties felt an especial pride in this regiment, as it was almost wholly composed of men and officers from their limits. Our regiment was made up of men of character and*

Freedom Sanborn kept a diary from 1862 to 1864.

good standing, who enlisted because the country needed them to suppress the rebellion. No regiment left the State with men of finer personal appearance, or of more gentlemanly bearing, and it sustained a high reputation for honor and sobriety.

On Monday, September 22, we bid goodbye to the town folks, and we traveled to Concord via the railroad. The following day we received the rest of out State bounty.

Thursday, 25th, Col. Joseph H. Potter, U.S.M.A, from Concord took command of the regiment—we had inspection from 4–to 6 pm, and the following day had our colors presented to us and got orders to leave for Washington the next day.

I was very impressed with the Colonel for he was a graduate of West Point in the class of 1843. After graduation, became to Brevet Second Lieutenant First Infantry on July 1, 1843; attached to the Seventh Infantry in 1845; severe wounded in the battle of Monterey in September 21, 1846. He was decorated for his "gallant and meritorious conduct in the battle of Monterey, Mexico."

After several years of commendable service, Colonel Potter was appointed to the Twelfth New Hampshire Volunteer Regiment in September 1862, assuming command on September 21. During the Battle of Chancellorsville, he was severely wounded and taken prisoner on May 3, 1863. He received honors for "gallant and meritorious service at the battler of Chancellorsville, Virginia" and was brevetted brigadier general in the United States Army in March 1865.

On Saturday, September 27th, the regiment was recruited and staged at Concord. With a strength of 1,019 officers and enlisted, the regiment left Concord for Washington at 8 o'clock. We passed through Manchester and Nashua en route to Worcester; we got dinner and continuing. We passed through Norwich and took the Steamer City of New York *at Allyn's*

Point—went across the sound, and got to Jersey City at 2 o'clock; left there at 8:30.

On Sunday the 28th, we passed through Trenton and finally arrived in Philadelphia at 3:00 pm.

On Monday, the 29th, the regiment left at 6 o'clock and arrived in Baltimore at 3am. Got our breakfast then waited until 2 pm to continue our trip for Washington. We heard that one man was shot soon after leaving Baltimore. Shortly thereafter we joined Colonel Wright's division of General Casey's command of the Reserve Army Corps, Defenses of Washington. The Regiment went by the "cars" to within a short distance of Harpers Ferry where we joined the Army of the Potomac in its march to Falmouth Heights opposite Fredericksburg on the Rappahannock River.

"Hurry up and wait!" It seems like all we do is drill, drill, and more drilling. We've been held up at camp for nearly two months and the waiting is taking its toll.

Subsequently, we were assigned to General Whipple's division, Third Army Corps, and with it marched from Berlin to Potomac Creek, near Falmouth, Virginia a distance of more than a hundred miles, arriving there on the 25th of November.

Needless to say we suffered from poor diet and consequently, from poor health, particularly during these winter months. Unaccustomed to camp life, many of the men became sick from exposure, short rations, jaundice and measles. The latter, in most cases, proved fatal, or caused permanent disability.

The food was poor and what government rations are available, it will never replace home cooking. With only tents to protect us against the cold and snow, the men face increased risk of pneumonia in this God forsaken Virginia camp. Most of us had less to fear from bullets than from disease. During these campaigns, physicians knew little for the care and cure of the soldiers. One soldier wrote:

"The Regtl. Surg., our Chaplain & my Son done all they could for me. They kept me hot bricks to my feet & hot cloths on my stomach but the Cold clamy Sweat ran out at every poar—cold as death. Oh such hours of suffering, but the Lord was with me, praise his holy name."

The lack of fresh fruit and vegetables also led to rampant scurvy among the troops. Eating raw and rotten meat often produced digestive disorders. Most soldiers did their own cooking by frying everything. With little cooking experience and few ingredients, some unique dishes were created. Coosh, or slosh, was cornbread, cornmeal or flour mixed with water until the mixture flowed like milk. It was fried in boiling grease until the water boiled off, and then it resembled dirty brown hash. Ashcakes were made of cornmeal mixed with salt and water and then wrapped in cabbage leaves and cooked in the hot ash until firm. Sometimes, dried vegetables were doled out to the troops in two-inch-thick cakes, called "desiccated vegetables" or "baled hay" by the men. The cakes looked like a "dirty brook with dead leaves floating around" when mixed with water.

Sanborn continued:

> *Time passed at our encampment and on Saturday morning, November 15th, the regiment had orders to get ready to move in light march to Fredericksburg.*
>
> *They buried one poor fellow today with his drawers and shirt on—Benjamin Weeks of from Sanbornton—Co. D, 12th New Hampshire, died of disease at Potomac Creek, November 1862.*
>
> *My health is good and I hope it will continue so. I do not fear a battle half so much as I do of being sick. I shall be glad when this cursed rebellion is stopped. I do not think it will be settled by fighting.*
>
> *Thanksgiving brought little heart to enter into any celebration. There was great suffering in camp; food & weather being what they are. We had heavy frosts frequently, and many, having no blankets, were obliged to find warmth in exercise. My buddy and I had small blankets each, but even with these it was almost impossible to keep from freezing. We now sleep in the middle of turns, and this privilege is a matter of the gravest importance. The one who slept in the middle was usually quite comfortable, although his sphere of operation was rather limited, for those on the outside naturally inclined to crawl away from the chilly flanks toward the center. In this way we could get some sleep one night out of three, if not drowned out by a rainstorm.*
>
> *One highlight of the week was when fighting Joe Hooker reviewed our division. We had to march 2 miles for review; got news that there is to be no more fighting for 15 days—hope it is so…*
>
> *Wednesday, December 10th. We finally got orders to march. Left our knapsacks and marched over toward Fredericksburg. We began crossing the river—we met with little opposition. The Union volunteers crossed in boats and cleared the town. We tried all day to cross the river, but never did it. It was almost dark, and General Burnside suspended operations for the day.*

The Twelfth New Hampshire Volunteer Regiment at the bombardment of Fredericksburg, December 11, 1862.

On December 12, General Burnside's orders were for Franklin and Hooker to make the main attack, while Sumner would make a secondary attack on Maryne's Heights. Between them, it was hoped, they could push the Confederates off the ridge overlooking the town. We find ourselves in a battle at Fredericksburg. We are lying on our arms, listening to the roar of the guns.

It is now 11 o'clock and we are within one mile of our batteries. The Rebels are hid from us by a hill. Oh, what a roar—there is not one-half second intermission. The noise resembles a big thundershower in haying season.

The Union artillery fired across the Rappahannock River at the Rebel troops who were hiding behind the walls along the waterfront of Fredericksburg. The Union advance had made me cross an open plain, cut by steep banked drainage ditch some thirty feet wide and six feet deep. At the foot of Maryne's Hill, a sunken road with stone retaining walls on either side formed a natural trench for Confederate riflemen.

Now the Rebel sharpshooters had stalled our troops by running off the engineers who had worked through the night building pontoon bridges. Suddenly, 36 of our cannons blasted away for an hour at the Rebel lines. The charge of our troops upon the Rebel fortification exposed the men to the *first of artillery on the Heights. But shots and shells, though raking their ranks, did not stop them. On they went to a slight rise, 150 yards to the front, where they reformed, and then charged.*

When the Rebels got there, the enemy was waiting and opened fire on us from their Batteries and sent the shots and shells flying around our ears rather faster than was agreeable, but the Rebels shelled us when we came in sight; killed one man, and wounded 3 men of Company B.

We are lying on the banks of the river now (3 o'clock), the Rebels are still throwing shells and we continued to dodge them. Burnside called on Hooker to resume the assault on the hill; Hooker decided to suspend the assault and withdraw his troops. This is too close for comfort. We finally laid down for the night.

A New Hampshire soldier from another regiment, on the opposite bank of the Rappahannock, recorded the shelling of the Twelfth New Hampshire Regiment:

They bombarded the city on Thursday and drove the Rebels out. We went over to the city on Friday morning [December 12]. We laid by the side of the river that day and night. There is a steep high bank along side the river and we laid closed down to the river so their shells went over us but some of them struck into the river. They killed many that afternoon that belonged to the 12th Regiment right at the edge of the pontoon bridge. We see the shell when it struck. There was a regiment coming over the hill and the Rebels throwed over and one struck right among them and it laid out three. I don't know whether it killed them or not. They carried them off in an ambulance. It is hard business to see them killed.

Sanborn continues his diary on Saturday, December 13:

Our troops crossed the river and was held in reserve in the city all day. Fighting could still be heard a little way out of the city. It was a hard battle, but appeared that neither side seemed to get the day.

On Sunday the 14th there was little fighting. The Rebel and Union batteries exchanged a few shots with little results. We laid in the streets of the city ready to move if wanted.

Come Tuesday night we was marched all over the city, first in one place and then in another. About daylight we marched across the bridge and back to our old camp.

The attack on Fredericksburg. *Courtesy of the National Military Park, Gettysburg, Pennsylvania.*

A buddy of mine, Cpl. Olaf Jewett, from Company E wrote home:

"The rebs retreat as fast as we advance. I have not been sick and hope I shant, for it is a bad place to be sick here. They take most everything as they pass along cattle and anything, they do not allow it but the boys will go and get what they want and run the risk of getting punished. The weather was bad last night. Our company was on picket that night. I shall be glad when this war is over with so I can come home once more if I am lucky enough to come out of it all right which I think I shall."

Corporal Jewett was killed at Chancellorsville on May 3, 1863.

When Hooker had relieved Burnside after the disastrous Fredericksburg campaign, he found the Army of the Potomac in a sorry state: desertion was increasing, and the army's own interior administration had deteriorated.

Sanborn continues relating the boredom and his camp duties:

For the end of '62 and a good part of '63 we saw little action. Same old thing—drill and picket and drill again.

Sunday, the 28th The Battalion held inspection and dress parade as usual. Chaplain preached to us from the text "Remember the Sabbath Day," and as soon as we got in from meeting, we were ordered to fix up our quarters fast.

Tuesday, the 30th—Grand Review at 2 o'clock, John P. Hale, U.S. Statesman, was present.

Wednesday December 31, 1862. We mustered for pay, but guess it will be some time before we get it.

Time is passing us buy and we are getting restless. We are waiting for nothing. Hooker realizes this and wants to take some action, especially for the moral of the troops.

Hooker is a boastful, ambitious man, and an intriguer, but he is brave and aggressive as a combat leader. Now, he has unexpectedly showed himself to be an able administrator and organizer. Training and discipline tightened and an efficient military intelligence organization has been established. Hooker reorganized his troops into seven infantry corps and one cavalry corps, which increased the effectiveness of our horsemen.

We had a grand review yesterday for Gen. Joseph Hooker—It was a splendid sight to see. We have boys come every day from the 5th, 6th and other New Hampshire Regiments.

1863

The opening of the military season of '63 found them firmly planted on the line of the Rappahannock—a mere post office in Spottsylvania County, Virginia. We had superior numbers (132,000); the Rebels numbered only 65,000. It was here that Jackson outflanked and turned our Regiment to the right, sweeping everything before him; here it was that he fell under a mistaken volley from his own lines. The battle was a Union defeat. General Hooker lost more than 16,000 men, and the Rebels loss was a little more than 12,000.

January 20–23 Of this Mud March, Pvt. Martin Haynes wrote: "Our Division left camp Tuesday noon in a pouring rain and accomplished about a mile and a half under difficulties. On Wednesday we tried again and managed about six miles. The mud was simply awful, and it was almost an utter impossibility to move the wagons and artillery at all. The Manchester Battery was straddled along the road, a gun here and a caisson there over a stretch of three miles. And that was the way everything on wheels was hung up."

Yesterday the Division made its way back to the old camp.

During this dreary winter after Fredericksburg and the mud march, General Hooker's problem was to restore morale, confidence and military discipline among the troops. The alarming depletion in troop strength was due to sickness and desertion. Of the appalling sickness rate and death from disease at this time, it was recorded by the Twelfth Regiment that "thousands died in the hospitals, many more in their quarter. One morning seven of the 12th lay dead outside of the regimental hospital and another died therein an hour or two later before the others were buried, making eight."

Sanborn enters his account of the suffering and exhaustion of the day:

Little time has passed and I find myself weak and exhausted this morning, with blood feverish and my system racked with pain, the result of yesterday's suffering march, for it was one of the most wretched days that I passed in service.

Nothing could have been lovely than the morning, but the sky was soon overcast with dark clouds, and one of the most fearful thunderstorms broke forth that I have ever witnessed, followed by a severe and drenching rain, which continued during our march—day and night. We were without shelter, or wood to build a fire, and were obliged to exercise constantly to keep from chilling.

It is recorded that as many as three hundred are marked absent without leave in a single day. This may have been slightly exaggerated, but the rate of desertion in the Confederate Army was fully equal to that of our troops.

With better rations, improved quarters, constant drilling, infrequent reviews, and above all the coming of spring, the morale, health, and discipline of our troops improved.

On April 27 we had a corps review in the forenoon, and got orders to be ready to move in at a moments notice.

From April 'til September our troops had been almost constantly engaged, each endeavoring to deal a fatal blow that was intended to drive the enemy back either upon Richmond or Washington. For both the North and South, public feeling had been wrought up to its highest pitch. General Meade, it was hoped by the Union, would prove himself equal to the emergency, and many prayers were sent daily for him and his weary but courageous army.

Diary of Freedom Sanborn

In planning his offensive, Hooker had the problem of crossing the Rappahannock against a dangerous opponent; it seems that Lee had carefully fortified the south bank from Port Royal to Bank's Ford, but Hooker knew he had a superiority in troop numbers because he had learned that Lee had sent Longstreet south with two divisions to guard the Virginia-Carolina coast. So Hooker began to revise his plan.

Lee himself had been planning an offensive movement in the Shenandoah Valley, but now the extent of Hooker's actions temporarily baffled him.

Sanborn continues his entry on April 29, 1863:

The next day, April 29, we were ready to move. On the 30th, our troops moved in the direction of Chancellorsville. Lee moved his troops closer to Fredericksburg and sent Anderson to occupy a position near Chancellorsville. By 3:00 p.m., Hooker had put three corps in Lee's rear near Chancellorsville, with two of our divisions close behind. We marched down the river about four miles and laid down for the night. The next morning the pontoons were laid across the river under heavy fire.

April 30—Heavy rain in the morning. Got a dispatch from Gen. Hooker that he had got in the rear of the Rebels and at noon got orders to march to the right and reinforce him. Hooker, however, halted his three corps to wait reinforcements.

At Chancellorsville was located a long brick house at a minor crossroads in a waste area appropriately called "the Wilderness." Thick second-growth pine and oak tangled with undergrowth severely limited visibility and made movement away from the few roads difficult; the area was further cut up but many swampy little streams, all of which militated against the deployment of our troops—our advantage was cancelled out. Nevertheless, Hooker delayed there until about 11:00 am.

May 1—After a 15 mile march this morning we crossed the river at Kelly's Ford and marched by the river for about 9 miles and attacked the Rebels about 5 pm—shelled them until dark then stopped 'til the next morning.

May 2—Our Regiment marched to the front line in the morning. For more than two days, the Rebels had held their position. Under the circumstances it was our custom to lie down after taking evening meal, not to sleep, but rather to talk over the events of our boyhood days, and life in general. Thoughts from home and the friends gathered around the firesides, there memories dwelt with clinging interest on scenes that might never be repeated; imagination feasted herself on pictures that might never prove a reality, and thus the long night was wearied through until the stars were growing dim in the light of approaching day.

There were but a few men among us who had even been compelled to suffer such privations and hardships. Before entering the army, most of us had been farmers from central New Hampshire, who had never known life in this manner. But most of us had offered their services to their bleeding, and distracted country, to assist in subduing the elements of discontent at the South, and the foulest and most unwarrantable rebellion against just and proper authority, ever known within the annals of time.

Rough terrain, hard fighting and a series of errors by subordinate commanders had taken most of the sting out of Jackson's attack, and the Rebels' rush was finally stopped west of Fairview Hill. Darkness fell, but Jackson, seeking a way to exploit his success, rode out into the gloom of night with a small entourage searching for a route that would enable him to cut Hooker off from United States' Ford. Returning, Jackson was shot down by his own men, who were jumpy from an earlier chance clash with our cavalry. Soon, the Confederate operation against our right came to a confused halt. Jackson died on May 10.

Sanborn continues:

At daylight, on the morning of the 3rd of May, General Whipple's division was formed in line at the foot of the hill, near the Chancellor House, and at right angles with the plank road. Gen. Hooker again had an excellent opportunity to defeat the Rebels. The Rebel Army around Chancellorsville was completely split with its two halves almost a day apart. Hooker repulsed the attack on the Rebels; furthermore he made no effort to regain the initiative, but instead ordered a second line of defense north of Chancellorsville. Hooker had visited Hazel Grove's high ground and should have appreciated that our attack from there would have struck the flank of Lee's army.

The foot cavalry was repulsed. Hooker, who had been actually incapacitated, ordered a withdrawal and his troops; spent a bloody day extricating them selves from the salient. At this time, the 12th was extensively engaged. When the regiment reached the newly formed Union line, only about 25% of our number of that morning was present for duty and our only remaining officers were two lieutenants. One of the most desperate musketry engagements ensued which has ever been witnessed.

The regiment behaved splendidly and retreated in good order, just in time to save its entire capture. General Whipple was mortally wounded and, while being carried from the field on a stretcher, bleeding and dying, said, "I hope I may live long enough to give Colonel Potter and his brave men a just report."

The regiment went into the engagement in the morning with 28 officers and 549 enlisted men. It lost 3 commissioned officers, 15 commissioned officers wounded, 42 enlisted men killed, 212 enlisted men wounded, 51 enlisted men captured and 3 enlisted men missing, probably killed.

THE GETTYSBURG CAMPAIGN

After the Battle of Chancellorsville and the retreat of the army, under the command of General Hooker, the Twelfth Volunteer Regiment returned to the camp it had occupied the previous winter. It remained there until June 11, when it broke camp and went in pursuit of the Rebel army on its raid in Maryland and Pennsylvania.

In late May and early June, General Hooker had an inkling of Lee's plan, and he sent Sedgwick across the river to test the Confederate strength in the Fredericksburg area.

From here to Gettysburg, the march was the most severe of any ever performed by the Army of the Potomac. The men suffered from fatigue and excessive heat and were short on rations. Many of them fell out and died by the roadside.

In early June, Hooker began shifting his forces farther west. On June 13, certain that Lee was moving into the Shenandoah, he moved his army swiftly toward Manassas. According to Frederick Tilberg's *Gettysburg, National Military Park*, "By the 17th of June, The Rebels were strung out over a distance of one hundred miles, and by the 24th of June, they had closed up north of the Potomac. On that day, Hooker set his troops in motion toward Frederick, Maryland."

According to Tilberg:

> *During the night, the Union troops had strengthened an already strong position, and Lee, judging this to be an indication that Hooker intended to remain on the defensive, decided to concentrate against Sedgwick in hopes of destroying his corps. All three New Hampshire Regiments (2nd,*

Battle of Gettysburg on Cemetery Ridge, July 1–3, 1863.

5ʰ and 12ᵗʰ), participated in this campaign, which culminated at the Battle of Gettysburg.

Lee now decided to crush Hooker, even though Hooker was embedded in a formidable mass of field fortifications. Lee concentrated all his troops for an assault at sunrise, but Hooker had already decided on a withdrawal. The withdrawal took Lee completely by surprise, and only a few advance scouts ever-made contact with our troops.

On June 27ᵗʰ, Hooker had the army concentrated between Frederick and South Mountain, and had ordered cavalry sent forward towards Emmitsburg and Gettysburg. It was apparent that he had planned an operation against Lee's line of communication but had issued no definite orders. The Union troops could not afford another Chancellorsville, especially one fought on Yankee soil, so the Union Army gave Hooker all available reinforcements, including a large part of Washington garrison, yet Hooker was complaining that he was undermanned, and asked to be relieved. To our surprise, Lincoln accepted and Meade became the new commander of the Army of the Potomac.

Meade was a cautious fighter and fully aware that he was about to face Lee and his Confederate force. He realized the enormous burden that rested on his shoulders. On the 30ᵗʰ of June, Meade's determination weakened.

He lost sleep, missed meals, frequently changed orders, and many times became highly agitated. Was Meade really prepared to meet the Rebels?

It is important to know the terrain around Gettysburg for it shaped the battle. Intelligence, troop force and the prepared use of the high ground; these elements were in our favor.

Northwest of Gettysburg is the dominating height of Oak Hill, southward from which ran two high ridges: Seminary Ridge, the longer one, extends to the Peach Orchard and along the Emmitsburg Road beyond: just to the left is McPherson's Ridge, wider but lower. North of Gettysburg, the ground is relatively open and level, while south of the town, Cemetery Hill rises abruptly some eighty feet. A lower ridge runs eastward from Cemetery Hill, ending in the rugged, wooded mass of Culp's Hill, while Cemetery Ridge extends for approximately a mile to the south. At its southern elevation is Little Round Top and Round Top. From Round Top to Culp's Hill, alone the "fishhook" line, is approximately four miles. Seminary Ridge and Cemetery Ridge run parallel, about a mile apart across open fields, whereas the ground between Seminary Ridge and Round Top is rough and broken.

Returning to Sanborn's diary, the following entries were made on July 1, 1863:

On July 1ˢᵗ we marched through Emmitsburg to within 2 miles of Gettysburg. The battle had begun at 8:00 a.m. July 1ˢᵗ.

When we met the enemy at Gettysburg it was a relief to many of us to know that they had an opportunity to fight rather than march, and all went forward determined to conquer the rebels or die in the attempt.

On Thursday evening, during the second day of battle [July 2, 1863], three New Hampshire regiments were heavily engaged. Our line was formed that morning under the command of Captain J.K. Langley. The engagement commenced in the afternoon. The Twelfth was stationed near the center of the line where the enemy made heavy attack. All through this bloody and decisive battle the regiment fought with great gallantry, fully sustaining the reputation that had won at the heavy cost at Chancellorsville.

Frederick Tilberg records the following:

After nearly three hours of the hardest fighting of the battle, it was favorable for the Rebels. They had won nearly all along the line and had gained possession of the summit of Little Round Top. From this point they were driven by Crawford's Division of the 5ᵗʰ Corps (a Pennsylvania Reserve) who, coming up fast, charged upon them with great fury, drove the Rebels down the rocky front of the hill, across the valley below, over the next hill, and into the woods beyond, taking more than three hundred prisoners.

Thoroughly driven back, and with several losses, the enemy made no further attempt upon our left wing, but the Rebel General Ewell, who commanded on the enemy's left (opposite our right) and had determined to obtain possession of Culp's and Wolf's hills to the right and southeast of Cemetery Hill, took advantage of the weakening of our right to support the attack of Longstreet and Hill on the left, massed his force first against the position of the 11ᵗʰ Corps on Cemetery Hill, and afterward on Green's Brigade of Geary's Division, which alone remained of the 12ᵗʰ, the rest having crossed to the support of the 3ʳᵈ Corps and which guarded the valley between Culp's and Wolf's Hill. Our troops were concentrating and confirming ourselves on the line of the Round Tops, Cemetery Ridge, and Culp's Hill.

Longstreet's attack was a jumbled affair from the very beginning; divisions went into battle piece meal, but with savage enthusiasm. Hood's division quickly smashed Sickles's left flank, over ran the Devil's Den, and went clawing up the west side of Little Round Top. This was the key to the Union position because, from the crest, fire could be directed down the whole of our line.

The Rebel forces made an oblique attack on the Union troops both at Little Round Top and Devil's Den. The area between these two positions, which became known as the "Slaughter Pen" was littered with bodies of Rebels who were felled by devastating volley of rifles and canister before we pulled back to the Devil's Den. During this day we had seen hard fighting. A sharpshooter's rifle had me in his sight. I received a bullet in the neck and was promptly taken prisoner. I laid in the woods all day near the hospital.

Dead from both armies littered the landscape, and it was over a week after the battle ended before all the bodies were removed and buried.

The losses during the day's fighting had been very severe on both sides, but they were heaviest on the side of the Rebels. With the exception of the slight advantage gained at Sprangler's Spring, which proved to be of no subsequent importance, they had been repulsed with great loss in their attempt to carry every point. They were not defeated, however, and the reinforcements that they had received during the day had yet taken no part in the fighting. Together with the fact that a retreat could only prove ruinous

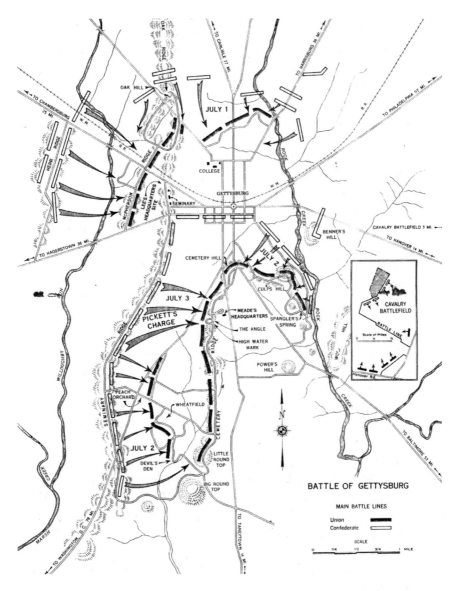

Map of the Battle of Gettysburg. *Courtesy of the National Military Park, Gettysburg, Pennsylvania.*

to their cause, the Rebel commanders resolved to continue the assault on the next day, July 3. Lieutenant Richard S. General Ewell's corps was assigned the task of carrying the Union right wing, and to Longstreet that of breaking the Union left center, the weakest point of its lines.

On the eve of July 2, General George E. Meade took council with his corps commanders: should they withdraw, or should they fight? His commanders voted to stay, and so Meade placed Hancock in charge.

Tilberg recorded:

Longstreet urged Lee to reduce the Union left, get across Meade's line of communication and force him to attack. Lee knew he had little time. He could not delay and maneuver because his army was living off the country, and would soon strip it bare: his own communications were highly vulnerable, and besides, the enemy in front of him engaged his natural combativeness. He gave his orders: Longstreet would penetrate the Federal center, while Stuart with all the army's cavalry, would strike the enemy's rear. Longstreet protested, but made the necessary preparations. He had 159 guns massed opposite the Union center, and about 15,000 infantry troops under Pickett readied for the assault. At 1:00 pm, the Confederate artillery open up, and was answered by only a brief Union artillery response (they had stopped to conserve ammunition), and, believed they had won the duel, urged Pickett to advance while they could still support him. As Pickett's men advanced, Union cannons tore huge gaps in their ranks, and Union infantry attacked their flanks. Yet they crashed into the first Union line. Then the Federal forces closed in. Well behind the battle, Brig. Gen. David M. Gregg intercepted Stuart and drove him back. Although urged to counterattack after Pickett's attack had failed, Meade was content to fight defensively.

Pickett's charge was a disaster. Both armies were badly mauled; the Union lost 23,049 killed, wounded and missing—approximately 25 percent of its total force. The Rebels reported losses totaling 20,451, although their returns are incomplete. It is more likely that their actual losses were 28,000, about one-third of their troops. Lee accepted the blame for Pickett's defeat: "It was all my fault," he told the survivors.

Frederick Tilberg's *Gettyburg* enters the following closing remarks of the Battle at Gettysburg:

On the 5th of July the Rebels skedaddled and our troops advanced. The rebel army having retreated, the pursuit again commenced and a long march was ensued.

The season was well consumed, yet no decisive results were apparent. It is true that the Rebel invasion of Pennsylvania had proven a failure, and Gettysburg had been a bloody turning point of the war. The ranks of

Lee's army had been somewhat thinned by desertions and much shattered by unprecedented casualties in battle. Nevertheless, he still presented a very strong front, indicative of much of the un-wasted energy. On our side active preparations were in progress for a renewal of the struggle. Pickett's line along the front were reinforced with orders to be unusually vigilant. Reconnaissances were frequent, and scouts were busy in all directions—a general advance was confidently expected. Not just on the eve of movement, intelligence was received that Lee suddenly withdrew the main force from the line of Rapidan and was making a rapid flank movement, which threatened the occupation of the plains of Manassas before Meade could reach them. Swift couriers from officers high in command brought orders to retire with promptness, but in good order if possible.

Returning to Sanborn's diary, he concludes with brief remarks of his service with the Twelfth Volunteer Infantry Regiment:

Eventually, I had my wounds dressed by a Rebel Surgeon, and took my leave of the Rebels and came to my regiment. They placed me in Division Hospital.

The next morning, July 8th, I was sent off with seven others of our regiment to Gettysburg to take the cars for Baltimore. I got on the train about 6 pm, but did not go a single inch that night. Left Gettysburg at 10 am, passed through Hanover and York. We arrived in Baltimore at about 2 o'clock the next morning.

On the 10th I left Baltimore at 9 am for Philadelphia and arrived there at 5 pm where I was carried to the West Philadelphia Hospital.

On the 19th I was still in the hospital. No change of getting a furlough yet. This is worse than a prison, there is a guard on duty all the time.

I am totally sick and tired of this. Wish I were well enough to return with the regiment.

July 26—The clerk came over and made out my furlough yesterday.

July 29—Got my furlough at 4 pm and started out at once. Got to New York at 10 pm, and went to the soldier's relief room—194 Broadway.

July 30—I remained in New York for the day. I went to see the Barnum Museum, and started from there at 5 pm on the steamboat Commonwealth.

The next morning—July 31, I arrived in Boston at 6 am, at Concord at 10:30, and finally at Laconia. Father met me and we rode home together. When we arrived, every one was glad to see me—I'm glad to get home once more. It's Sunday and the whole family and I went to meeting and heard preacher in the forenoon, afterwards we went to Laconia.

August 4 and the folks are busy haying. I can't do much so I don't try.

On the 10th I went to Concord to get my furlough extended—no luck! However, the next day I had to report to Concord.

On the 24th I was examined and marked to go to the regiment.

On the 27th I was ordered to go to the city with those who were going to the regiment. Saw the major and he took my name off the paper and said I need not go at this time. Here I laid around the barracks.

Finally, I was examined again and was marked for the Invalid Corps. In the meantime I returned home on a four-day pass.

Sept 10th—I took the first train for Concord; left there at 9 o'clock for New York. I arrived in New York at 9 a.m. I was immediately transferred to Governor's Island and waited for transportation to the regiment. While on the island, I just waited and watched the ships passing by.

Sept. 16th—I went on board the steamer Atlantis. At 5 in the afternoon we all left for Alexandria.

For two days at sea, a tremendous storm blew the steamer around like fury. I got pretty sick. The steamer anchored in the mouth of the Chesapeake Bay. The next morning we went up to the mouth of the Potomac and arrived at Alexandria at noon.

Promptly I was sent over to the convalescent camp.

Sept. 21st—I was transferred to Point Lookout. Upon arrival at 5 o'clock I was assigned to work cutting lumber. I spent much or the week working in the wood.

Oct. 3rd—I have been at work all this week building a blockhouse on the neck—got it about half done.

Oct. 22nd—The steamer Ashland arrived at camp with 1,000 Rebel prisoners for us to guard—this makes about 6,000 that are in our care.

For the next two week I spent most of my time writing home and working on the Guard House.

Nov. 13th—The 5th New Hampshire came here from Long Island—a very refreshing change.

Nov. 19th—I finally finished a room on the Guard House and put the remaining Rebel prisoners in it.

Nov. 26th—I finally had a good Thanksgiving dinner; received a letter from father and wrote home.

Dec. 12th—The Regiment was paid off—I got $596.00—I sent $80.00 home in Sanbornton.

For the next few days I spent working in the Rebel camp.

Dec. 19th—It was my 22nd birthday and worked in the woods—it was damn cold.

Dec. 25th—Christmas was uneventful—had a good dinner and fine fellowship with my buddies.

Dec. 31st—We mustered for pay. The old year has most gone. I have been through a good deal and have seen some things that I had rather not seen.

Memorandum
December 29, 1864
The year is drawing to a close and I will look it over a little. At the beginning of the year I was a soldier in the 12th New Hampshire at Point Lookout, MD; had served about a year and six months and it looked likely enough that I should serve the whole of my time out (3 years), but the last of January 1, 1864, I was discharged on account of the loss of my voice caused by a wound in the throat received at the Battle of Gettysburg the July before. I went home about the 9th of February and stayed about home until after haying time then went to Vermont to see Lydia and from there I went to Springfield with Leonard and stayed there a month tending his horses; then came home.

About the first of July, I began to recover my voice. It was very weak at first, but it grew stronger by use and now it is most as strong as ever.

In the month of June and July there was severe drought and everything looked as though we should not raise anything; but the last of July it began to rain and after that we had rain enough and our crops came in better than we expected so we have enough of everything.

The work of putting down the rebellion has progressed well and I hope before long the Rebels will be brought into subjection and the war will close. Richmond can't hold out much longer, and when that comes down the rebellion will be about played out.

Freedom Sanborn
Co. H 12th Regiment
Point Lookout, Maryland

On October 1, 1873, Freedom Sanborn died of a heart disease induced by his military service.

Bibliography

Abbott, John S.C. *Civil War in America*. Springfield, MA: Gurdon Bills, 1866.

The American Soldiers and Sailors in War. A Pictorial History. N.p.: Edward J. Stanley, Publisher, n.d.

Anderson, Hilary, and W. Jeffrey Bolster. *Soldiers, Sailors, Slaves and Ships. Civil War Photography by Battles and Leaders of the Civil War*. Grant-Lee edition, vols. I–VI. New York: Century Company, 1899.

Cleveland, Mather, MD. *New Hampshire Fights the Civil War*. New London, NH, 1969.

Garrison, William Lloyd. *Liberator* (newspaper), 1864.

Great Battles of the Civil War. N.p.: Time Inc., 1961.

Harpers Pictorial. *The Civil War*. New York: Harper Brothers, 1866.

Heald, Bruce D. *Images of the Civil War*. Charleston, SC: Arcadia Publishing Company, 2001.

Henretta, James A., and David Brody. *America: A Concise History*. 4th edition. Boston: Bedford/ St. Martins, 2010.

Moore, Henry P. *The New Hampshire Historical Society*. Concord, New Hampshire.

Pillsbury, Hobart. *New Hampshire: A History*. New York: Lewis Historical Publishing Company, 1927.

Schmucker, Samuel. *The History of the Civil War in the United States*. Chicago, 1865.

Tilberg, Frederick. *Gettysburg, National Military Park*. National Park Service Handbook Series 9, 1961.

Waite, Otis F.R., Major. *New Hampshire in the Great Rebellion*. Claremont, NH: Tracy, Chase & Company, 1870.

Wiley, Bell Irvin. *The Life of Billy Yank, the Common Soldier of the Union*. New York: Bobbs-Merrill Company, 1952.

Index

About the Author

Dr. Bruce Heald is a graduate of Boston University, the University of Massachusetts at Lowell and Columbia Pacific University. He is presently an adjunct professor of American military history at Plymouth State University and a fellow in the International Biographical Association and the World Literary Academy in Cambridge, England. Dr. Heald is the recipient of the Gold Medal of Honor for literary achievement from the American Biographical Institute (1993). From 2005 to 2008, he was a state representative to the General Court of New Hampshire. He resides in Meredith, New Hampshire, with his family.

Dr. Heald has written several books on the history of New Hampshire and wishes to preserve and write the legacy of the Civil War through the soldiers' letters and diaries.

Visit us at
www.historypress.net